Brighter Child®
An imprint of Carson-Dellosa Publishing LLC
Greensboro, North Carolina

Brighter Child®
An imprint of Carson-Dellosa Publishing, LLC
P.O. Box 35665
Greensboro, NC 27425-5665

carsondellosa.com

ISBN 978-1-60996-982-0

01-153127784

Table of Contents

Table of Contents

A Big Walrus

Directions: Connect the dots from **15** to **43**. Then, color to finish the picture.

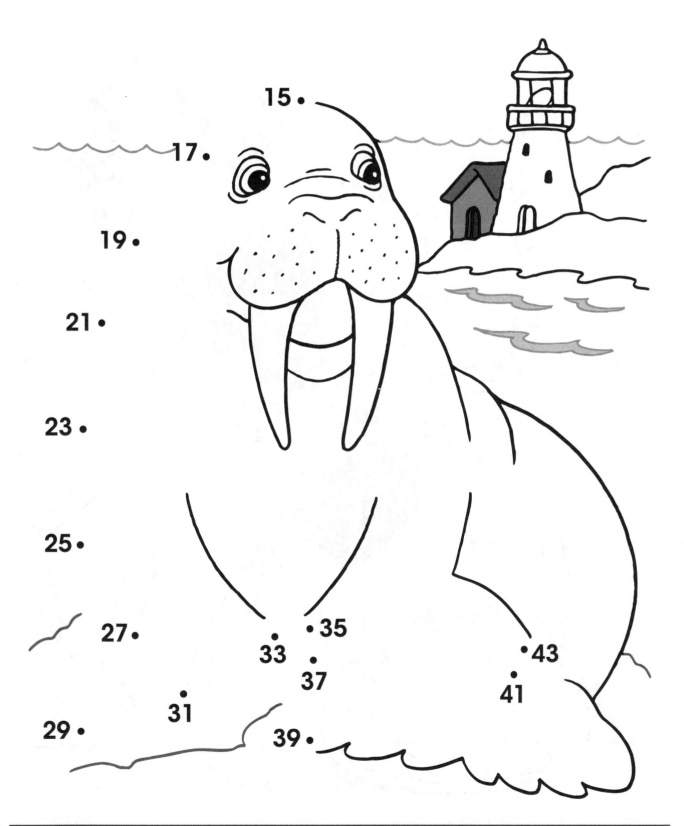

Vera the Velvet Ant

Directions: Connect the dots from **5** to **65**. Then, color to finish the picture.

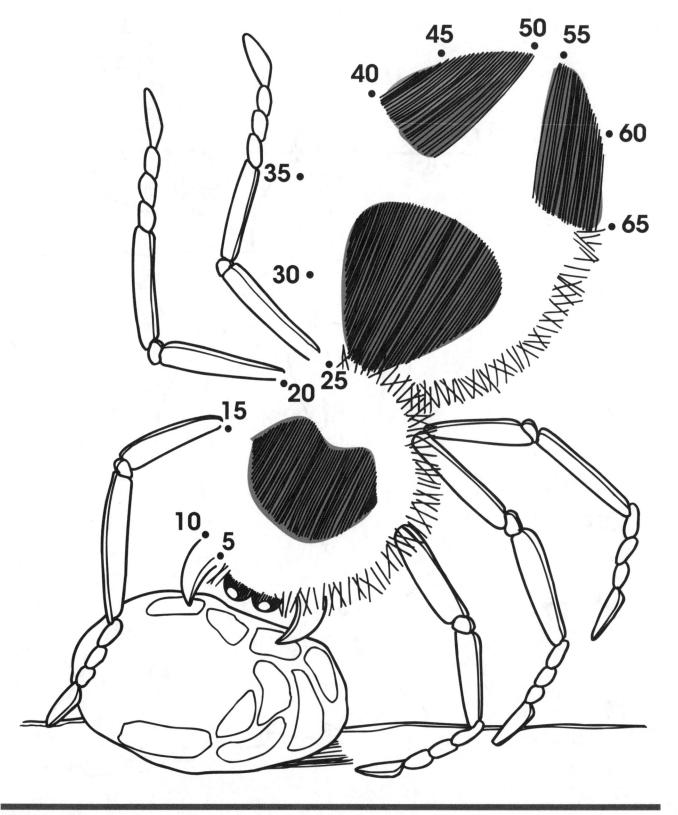

Hot and Cold

Directions: Read the clues. Then, find and circle the words in the puzzle.

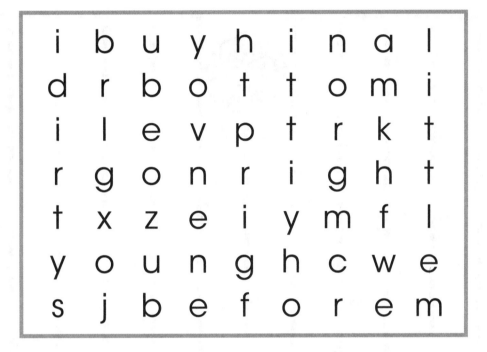

```
i  b  u  y  h  i  n  a  l
d  r  b  o  t  t  o  m  i
i  l  e  v  p  t  r  k  t
r  g  o  n  r  i  g  h  t
t  x  z  e  i  y  m  f  l
y  o  u  n  g  h  c  w  e
s  j  b  e  f  o  r  e  m
```

Opposite of **after**.
Opposite of **big**.
Opposite of **old**.
Opposite of **clean**.
Opposite of **left**.
Opposite of **top**.

Bowling Fun

Directions: Help the bowling ball find the pins.

Sewing

Directions: Find and circle the words in the puzzle.

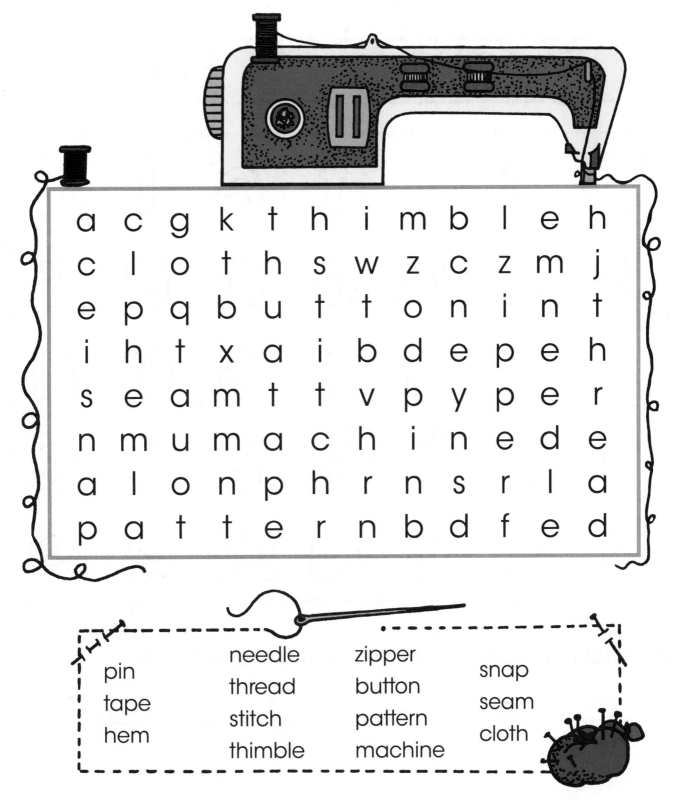

```
a c g k t h i m b l e h
c l o t h s w z c z m j
e p q b u t t o n i n t
i h t x a i b d e p e h
s e a m t t v p y p e r
n m u m a c h i n e d e
a l o n p h r n s r l a
p a t t e r n b d f e d
```

pin
tape
hem

needle
thread
stitch
thimble

zipper
button
pattern
machine

snap
seam
cloth

Mystery Sentence

Directions: Color the following words in the puzzle **green**.

| if | is | but | shoe | can | house | in |

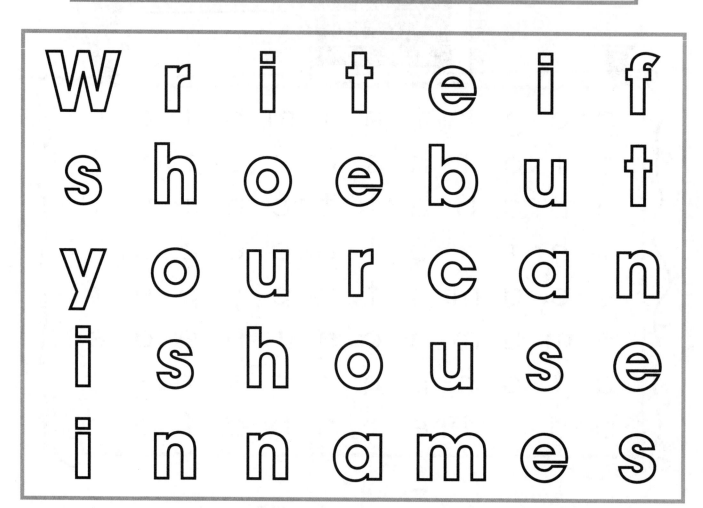

Write the words you did not color to make a sentence.

_____ _____ _____ .

Super Sleuths

Directions: Help the detectives find the magnifying glass. Then, color the picture.

Ages 7+

Fancy Fish

Directions: Connect the dots from **2** to **16**. Then, color to finish the picture.

Rico Rhinoceros

Directions: Connect the dots from **1** to **25**. Then, color to finish the picture.

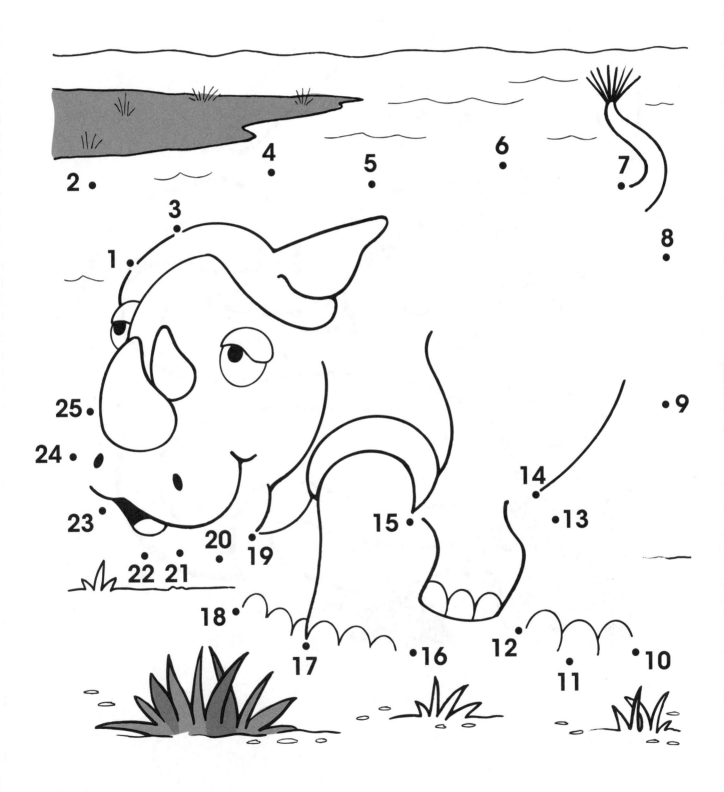

Ages 7+

Sweet Dreams

Directions: Find the path to the sleeping boy.

The Pied Piper

Directions: Connect the dots from **20** to **85**. Then, color to finish the picture.

Mail Call

Directions: Unscramble the words that have to do with mail. Use the words in the Word Box to help you.

1. rettles __ __ __ __ __ __ __

2. cpageksa __ __ __ __ __ __ __ __

3. tpamss __ __ __ __ __ __

4. ilam rrcaire __ __ __ __ __ __ __ __ __ __ __

5. tsop oceiff __ __ __ __ __ __ __ __ __ __

6. axombli __ __ __ __ __ __ __

7. leeydivr __ __ __ __ __ __ __ __

8. dracs __ __ __ __ __

delivery	mail carrier	
letters	stamps	packages
mailbox	cards	post office

What Shark Is This?

Directions: Connect the dots from **24** to **72**. Then, color to finish the picture.

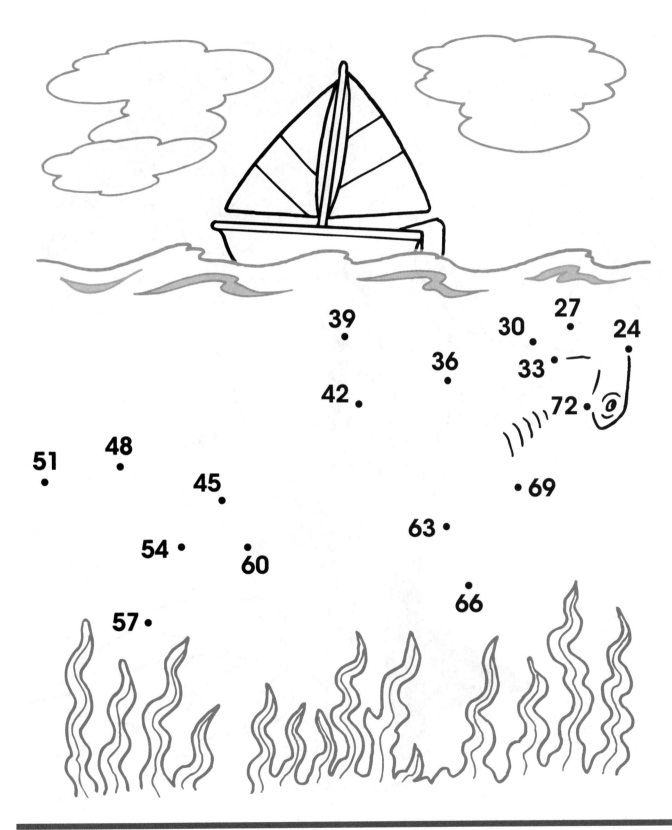

Thomas the Thorn Bug

Directions: Connect the dots from **0** to **35**. Then, color to finish the picture.

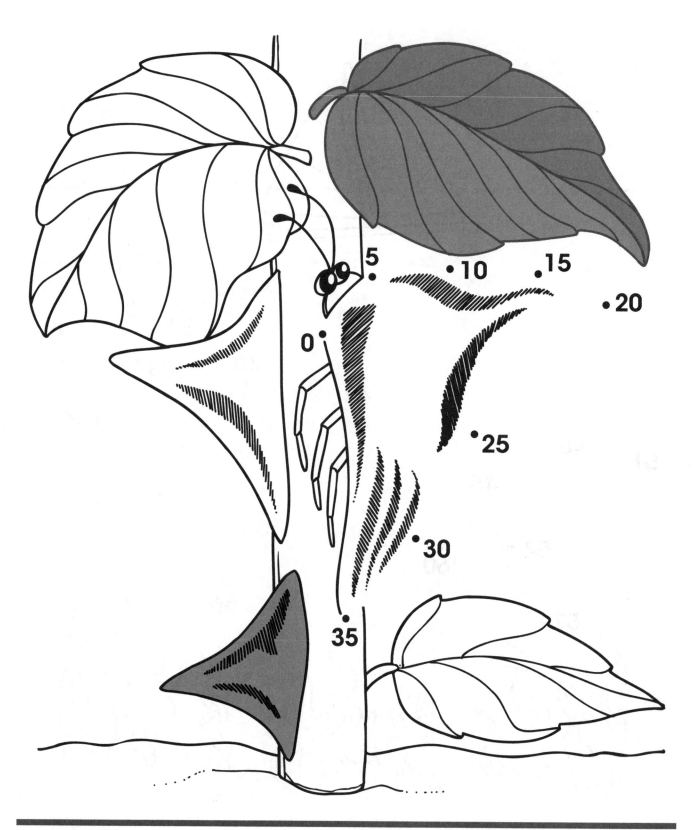

Yoli the Yellow Jacket

Directions: Connect the dots from **15** to **90**. Then, color to finish the picture,

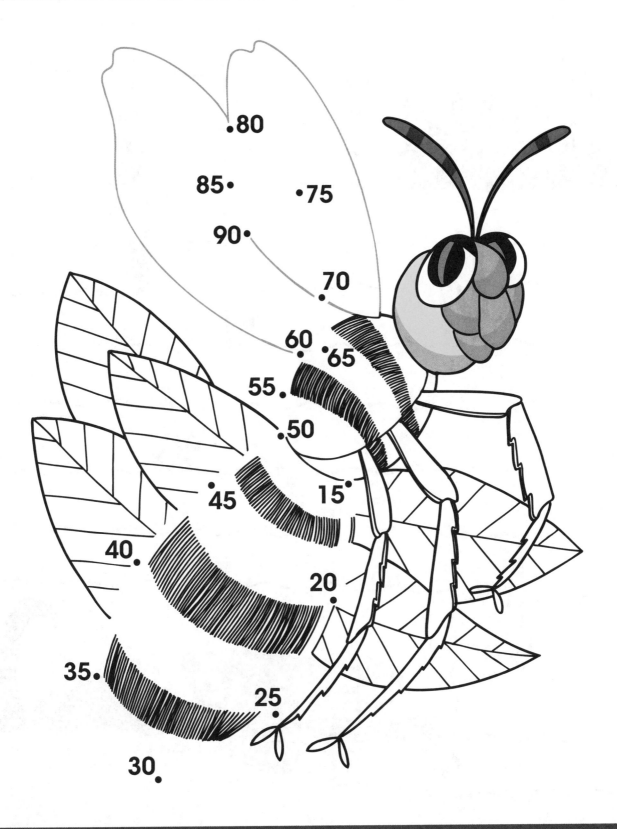

Ages 7+

Sun and Swim

Directions: Help the crocodile swim to the grassy bank.

Snow Sports

Directions: Find and circle the words in the puzzle.

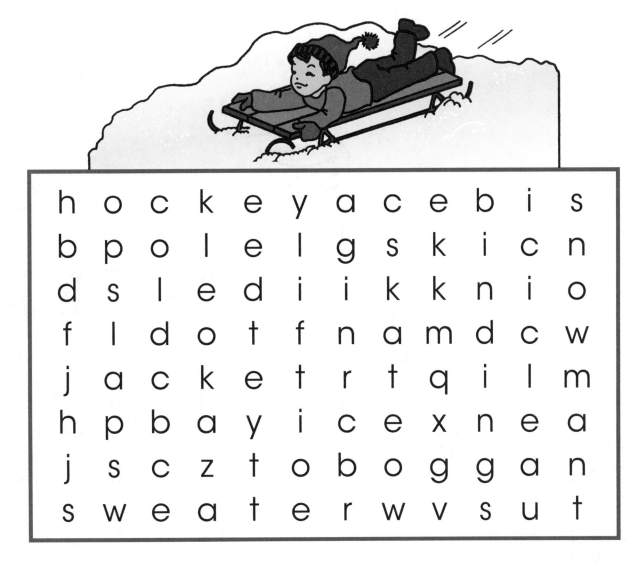

```
h o c k e y a c e b i s
b p o l e l g s k i c n
d s l e d i i k k n i o
f l d o t f n a m d c w
j a c k e t r t q i l m
h p b a y i c e x n e a
j s c z t o b o g g a n
s w e a t e r w v s u t
```

lift	ice	pole
skate	ski	sweater
icicle	hockey	bindings
jacket	snowman	toboggan
sled	cold	

Prince Charming

Directions: Connect the dots from **5** to **35**. Then, color to finish the picture.

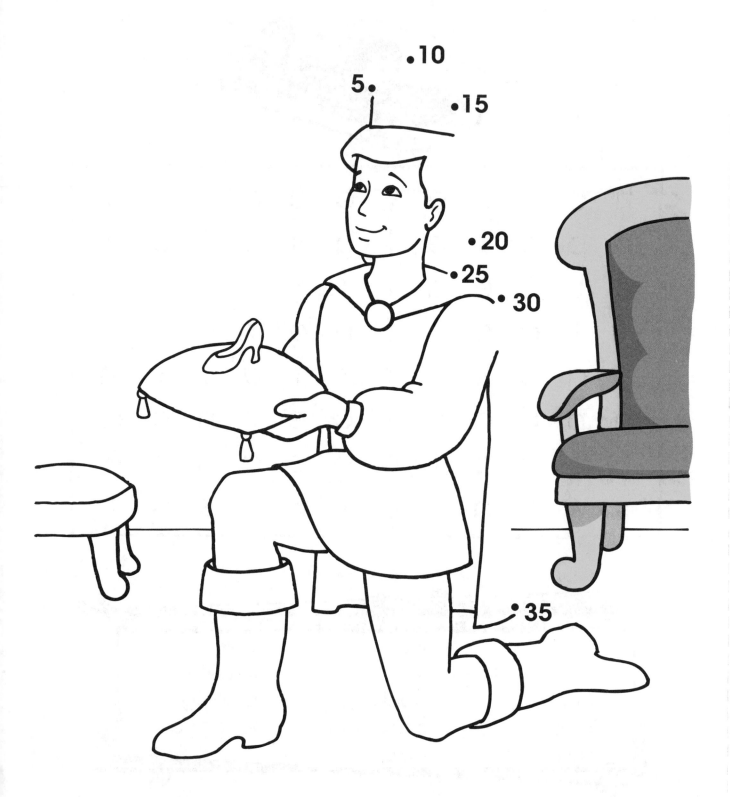

Art

Directions: Find and circle the words in the puzzle.

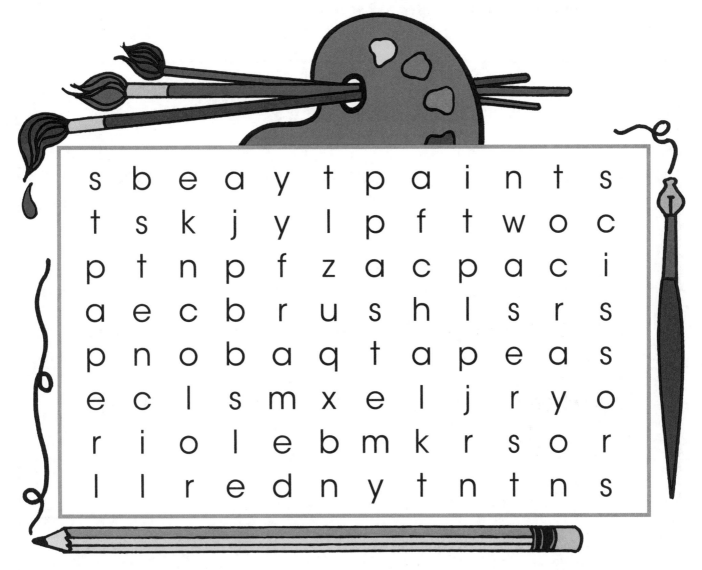

```
s  b  e  a  y  t  p  a  i  n  t  s
t  s  k  j  y  l  p  f  t  w  o  c
p  t  n  p  f  z  a  c  p  a  c  i
a  e  c  b  r  u  s  h  l  s  r  s
p  n  o  b  a  q  t  a  p  e  a  s
e  c  l  s  m  x  e  l  j  r  y  o
r  i  o  l  e  b  m  k  r  s  o  r
l  l  r  e  d  n  y  t  n  t  n  s
```

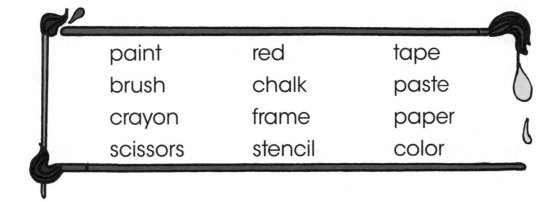

paint	red	tape
brush	chalk	paste
crayon	frame	paper
scissors	stencil	color

Color the Quilt

Directions: Read the words in the boxes. Then, color each box the color of the thing in the box.

sky	grass	sea
strawberry	ocean	cherry
river	lettuce	lake

Where's Walter?

Directions: Wilma's cat Walter is missing. Help her find him.

Lily the Ladybug

Directions: Connect the dots from **10** to **100**. Then, color to finish the picture.

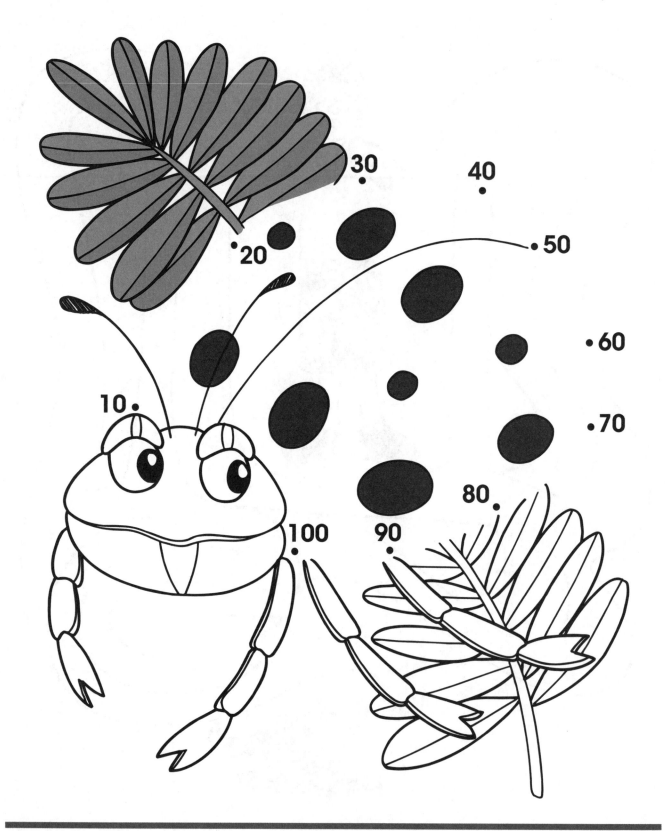

Carrie the Caterpillar

Directions: Connect the dots from **20** to **190**. Then, color to finish the picture.

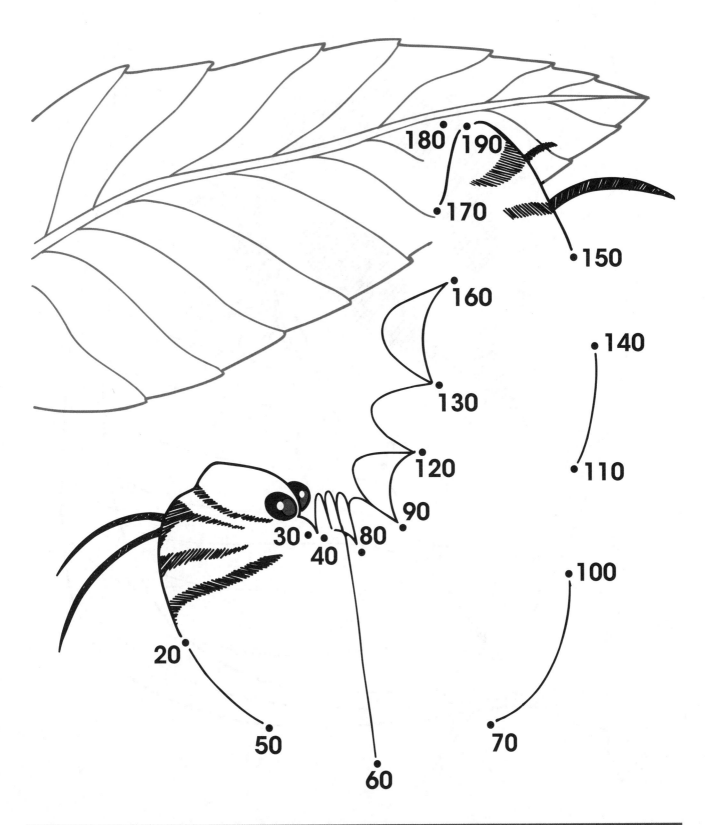

Taylor the Treehopper

Directions: Connect the dots from **0** to **65**. Then, color to finish the picture.

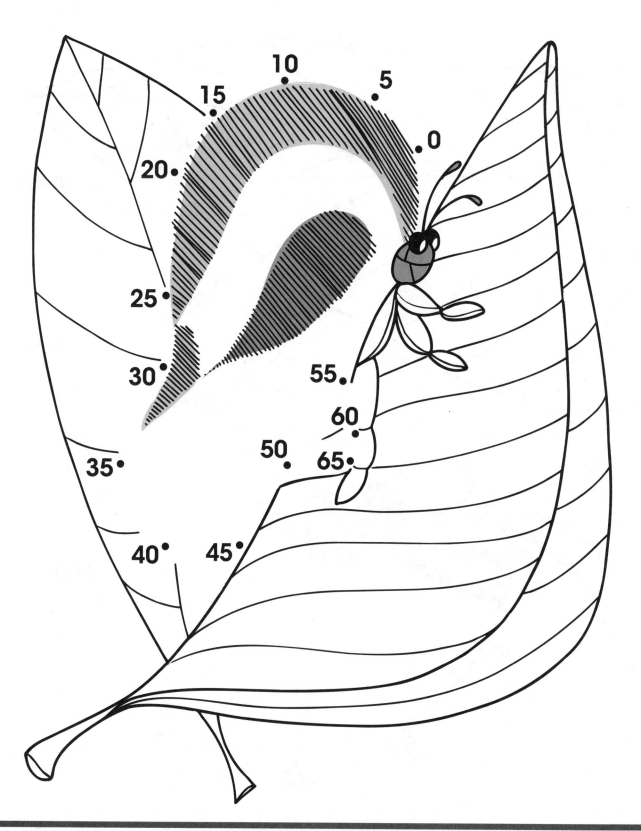

Dinosaur Riddles

Directions: Read each riddle. Draw a line to the matching picture.

I had a big head.
I had long, sharp
teeth.
Who am I?

Diplodocus

I had a big head.
I had three sharp
horns.
Who am I?

Parasaurolophus

I had a small head.
I had a long, long
neck.
Who am I?

Tyrannosaurus

I had a mouth like a
duck.
I had a long crest.
Who am I?

Triceratops

A Missing Slipper

Directions: Help the ballerina find her slipper. Then, color the picture.

Let's Fish

Directions: Help the fisherman find the fish. Then, color the picture.

What's the Word?

Directions: Find and circle the words in the puzzle.

```
y g h u p y t i d r e o n m t c
d y c y i b y e l l w g y u l e
b o t a s r e y e t n m a o m f
c w s r j f l a d g h o w s e o
x l y n l k l y e s t y n y a k
d y e h u p o y o u i m t a y y
v p a g e o w u n m j l u b i a
h k s o m p y o k e k m v c p m
g m t t c s y a r d c z y a p s
i l u r f k g u l f d u x o r e
```

yak	yawn	yes
yams	yeast	yet
yap	yell	yip
yard	yellow	yoke
yarn	yowl	yule
you		

Look and Write

Directions: Circle the names of things in the picture.

shuttle	clouds	stars
flowers	bicycle	lion
astronaut	stove	space suit
hot dog	moon	craters

Directions: Circle and write the best title for the picture.

Our Hot Sun　　　Working in Space　　　A Day at the Park

_____

Off to School

Directions: Color the letters **O** and **P** to find the path that leads to the bus.

Truckin' Along

Directions: Find and circle the words in the puzzle.

```
p  t  n  d  f  h  j  u  i  v  j  d  o  l  e
x  r  e  j  k  e  i  s  t  y  a  o  u  z  a
e  o  o  j  a  d  e  p  t  u  b  c  d  j  j
w  a  j  u  n  g  l  e  j  u  m  p  j  j  k
i  c  j  o  l  l  y  j  e  e  p  s  a  o  t
e  d  f  j  e  l  l  y  j  o  k  e  m  g  s
j  f  s  g  j  e  t  j  o  k  j  a  r  r  v
k  g  t  h  j  o  b  k  j  l  j  u  g  t  u
b  a  s  d  f  j  g  h  i  l  o  p  s  y  z
```

jump   jug   jolly
jade   jet   jog
joke   jungle   job
jelly   jar   jeeps
jab   jam

Spring

Directions: Read the clues and use the words in the Word Box to complete the puzzle.

Word Box:
buds
warmer
flowers
caterpillar
windy
rainy
kite
outdoors

Across

2. It is the opposite of **colder**.
3. These bloom in the spring.
6. You can fly one outdoors in the spring.
7. Trees have these in the spring.
8. Take your umbrella on days like this.

Down

1. This is busy eating new leaves in spring.
4. It's fun to play here.
5. This is a good day to fly a kite.

Apple Search

Directions: Help the elephant find more apples for her pie.

Insects

Directions: Find and circle the words in the puzzle.

```
f  l  y  b  u  t  t  e  r  f  l  y
e  l  b  u  t  e  t  b  e  r  b  z
e  e  y  g  t  u  p  d  r  p  e  q
l  g  r  a  s  s  h  o  p  p  e  r
e  s  z  t  c  r  i  c  k  e  t  o
r  r  a  n  t  v  w  a  s  p  l  a
s  t  i  n  g  e  r  c  p  u  e  c
w  i  n  g  s  p  t  v  m  o  t  h
```

fly	legs	wasp	ant
bug	beetle	cricket	wings
moth	roach	stinger	feelers
butterfly			grasshopper

Duck or a Dino?

Directions: Connect the dots from **4** to **40**. Then, color to finish the picture.

On the Moon

Directions: Circle the sentences that tell about the picture. Write them on the lines. Then, read the story.

They are on the moon.

The flag is flying.

There are tall green trees.

One astronaut is driving.

_____

_____

_____

Lock and Key

Directions: Help the key find the lock.

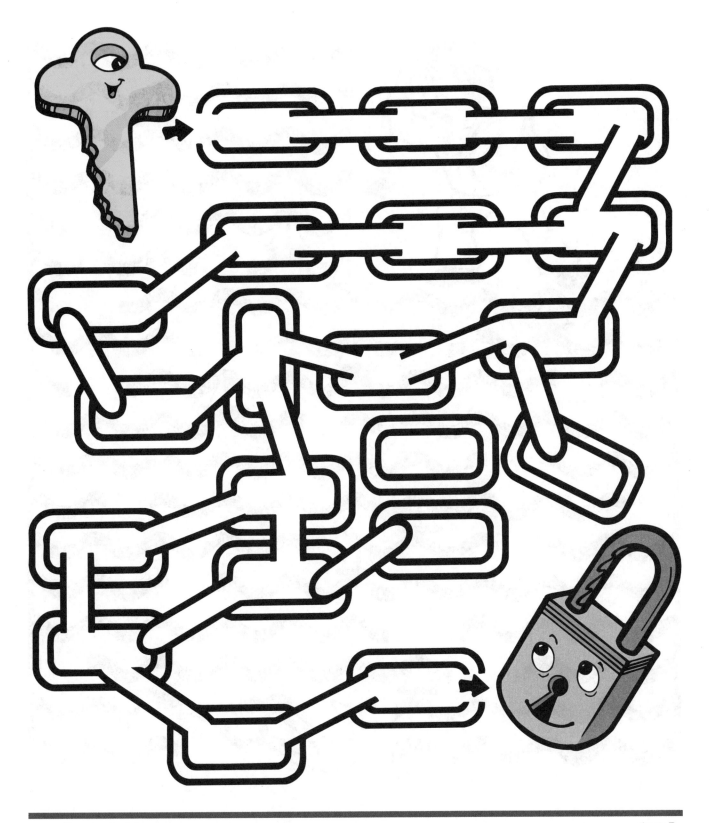

Sail Away

Directions: Help the sailor find the anchor.

Egg Hunt

Directions: Take the bunny to the decorated egg.

Around Town

Directions: Read each riddle. Then, write the answer. Use the words in the Word Box to help you.

play
work
vote
shop
learn
eat
help
drive

1. Kids do this with toys and at parks. ____ ____ ____ ____

2. People go to markets to do this. ____ ____ ____ ____

3. Teachers help kids do this. ____ ____ ____ ____ ____

4. You can do this at a restaurant. ____ ____ ____

5. People earn money by doing this. ____ ____ ____ ____

6. Adults travel in cars by doing this. ____ ____ ____ ____ ____

7. Do this to be a good neighbor. ____ ____ ____ ____

8. People do this to choose leaders. ____ ____ ____ ____

Sounds

Directions: Find and circle the words in the puzzle.

```
s p q n o s q u e a k u s
l b a n g d e y z x v w p
u u r i j f g c a p o s l
r z l k m c h b r q r t a
p z s t h u m p x a m l s
t s u t w l h i s s n h
q p u r r z y c b e d h j
u r x v w a s n a r l g k
c l i n k g r o w l f i h
```

bang   splash
buzz   squeak
crash   clink
growl   thump
purr   snarl
hiss   slurp

Time to Rake

Directions: Help John get through the pile of leaves.

Sizes

Directions: Find and circle the words in the puzzle.

```
c  q  r  g  i  g  a  n  t  i  c  y  z
o  t  m  n  l  k  j  b  h  b  x  t  a
l  s  s  h  o  r  t  i  i  c  w  i  l
o  p  m  o  u  v  a  h  u  g  d  n  i
s  z  a  x  c  b  w  v  u  g  e  y  t
s  y  l  a  t  a  l  l  t  g  p  f  t
a  h  l  d  k  t  l  a  r  g  e  o  l
l  m  i  n  i  a  t  u  r  e  n  q  e
f  g  i  e  m  j  s  g  i  a  n  t  r
```

big	little
colossal	miniature
giant	short
gigantic	small
huge	tall
large	tiny

Nice Hat!

Directions: Read the clues and use the words in the Word Box to complete the puzzle.

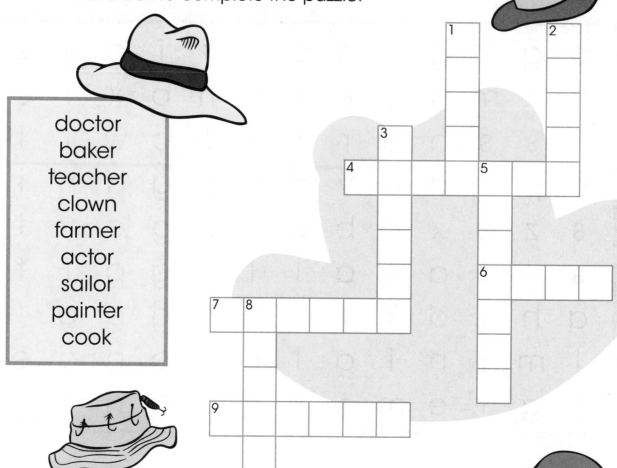

doctor
baker
teacher
clown
farmer
actor
sailor
painter
cook

Across

4. A person who paints.
6. A person who cooks food.
7. A person who sails.
9. The person who makes you well.

Down

1. A person who makes you laugh.
2. A person who bakes cakes.
3. A person who farms.
5. A person who teaches.
8. A person who acts.

A Long Fish

Directions: Connect the dots from **12** to **38**. Then, color to finish the picture.

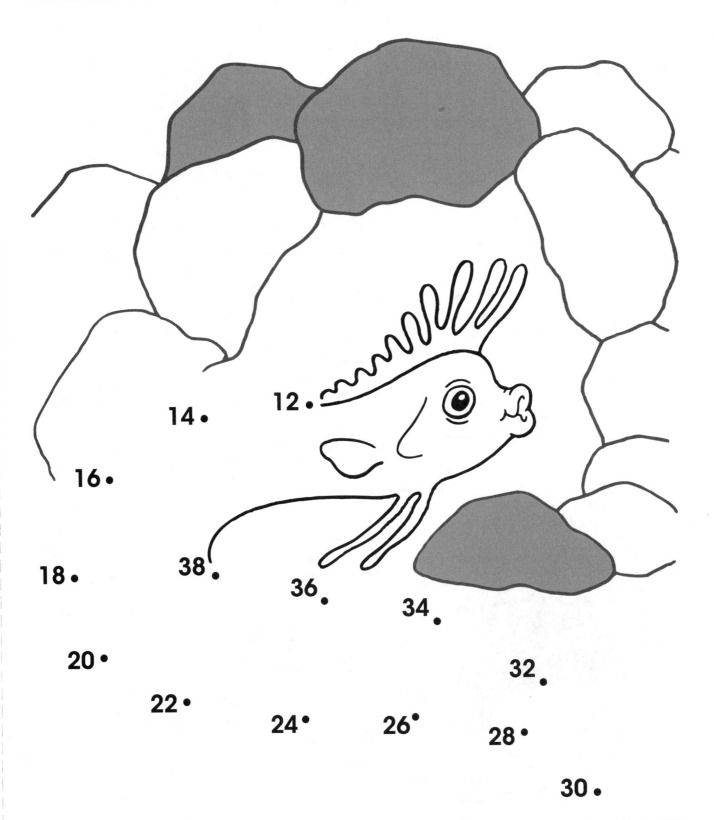

Ages 7+

Who Is Bigger?

Directions: Help the bear get home. Color numbers greater than **10**.

What Is It?

Directions: Color the spaces with words that name vehicles yellow. Color the other spaces **blue**.

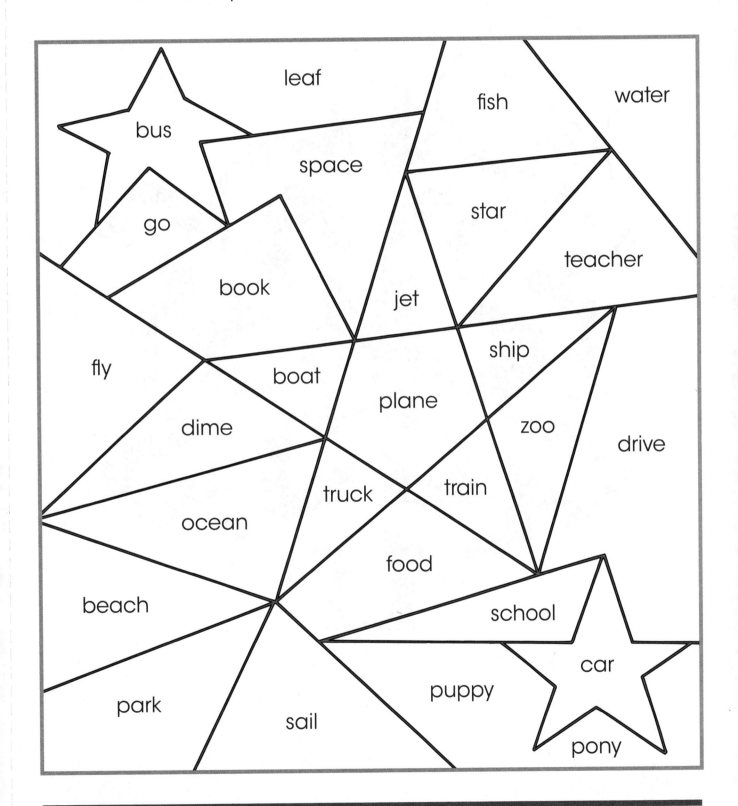

A Cold Place

Directions: Help the polar bear find the North Pole.

Making Music

Directions: Read the clues and use the words in the Word Box to complete the puzzle.

Word Box

drum
horn
violin
piano
guitar
note
music
listen
bells

Across
3. This instrument has black and white keys.
5. It is a musical sound.
6. You blow into this instrument.
7. Strike this instrument to make sounds.
9. Ring these to make sounds.

Down
1. You play the strings on this instrument with a bow.
2. People do this when they hear music.
4. An electric one is used for rock and roll.
8. It is another word for **beautiful sounds**.

Flowers

Directions: Find and circle the words in the puzzle.

```
m l l i l y a v i o l e t
a o j k p s e r d c b z a
l t i h f f e n i w y p p
s u n f l o w e r x t o a
b s c g o d d a i s y p n
r v s r p q n o s l m p s
u o t m a r i g o l d y y
f h s i d a f f o d i l k
e g d e c j b t u l i p a
```

rose
sunflower
iris
tulip

poppy
lily
marigold
violet

lotus
daffodil
pansy
daisy

The Magic Coach

Directions: Connect the dots from **4** to **80**. Then, color to finish the picture.

Mail Delivery

Directions: Lead the pig to the mailbox.

A Good Scout

Directions: Read the clues and use the words in the Word Box to complete the puzzle.

Across

1. A word you say when you get hurt.
3. The shape of a circle.
5. The opposite of quiet.
7. To find out how many, you must _____.
9. The opposite of **north**.
11. The opposite of **in**.
12. Animal like a rat.
14. A very high landform.

Down

2. Fluffy white object in the sky.
4. Ground wheat that is used in making bread.
6. Not having something.
7. A sofa.
8. A fish.
10. A home.
12. A part of your face.
13. To make a ball go down and up.

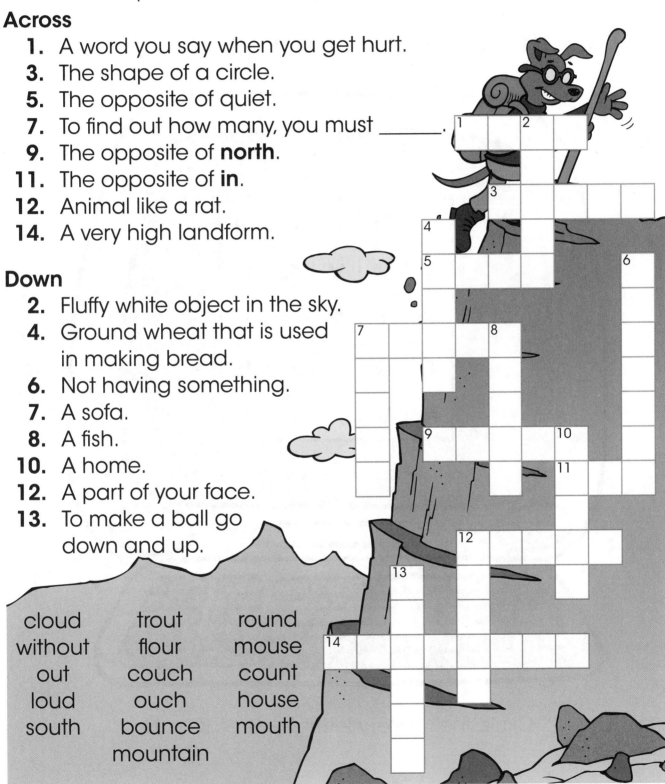

cloud	trout	round
without	flour	mouse
out	couch	count
loud	ouch	house
south	bounce	mouth
	mountain	

Keyboard Crazy

Directions: To find the mystery letter, color the spaces with the following letters **green**.

N   C   M   E   R   H   F   P   T   B   G   S   A

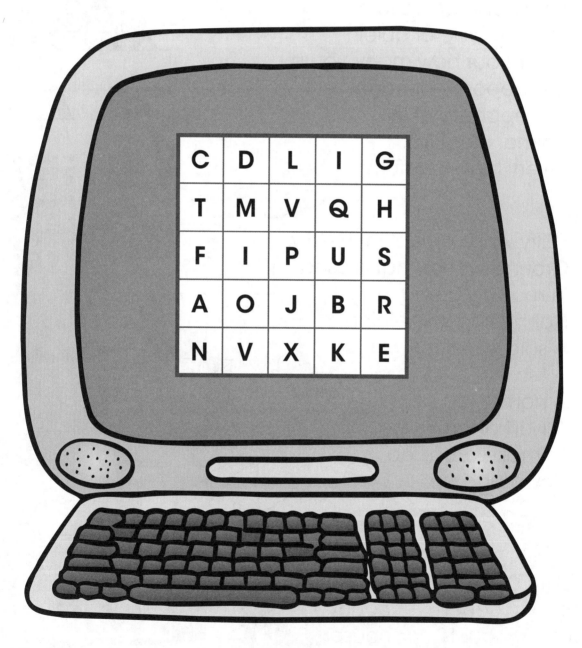

C	D	L	I	G
T	M	V	Q	H
F	I	P	U	S
A	O	J	B	R
N	V	X	K	E

Circle the mystery letter.   **B   K   N**

Camping Time

Directions: Help the Boy Scout find the tent. Then, color the picture.

The Gingerbread Man

Directions: Connect the dots from **0** to **24**. Then, color to finish the picture.

Moving to Music

Directions: Read the clues and use the words in the Word Box to complete the puzzle.

Word Box:
stretch
move
dance
leap
glide
step
skip
whirl
pose

Across

3. This is another word for **walk**.
6. You turn fast when you do this.
7. It is a jump.
8. You do this when you move to music.

Down

1. You do this when you go from one place to another.
2. Reach out and make your body fill more space.
3. You do this when you move with little leaps.
4. You do this when you stand very still.
5. This means **moving smoothly**.

A Smart Coral

Directions: Connect the dots from **9** to **54**. Then, color to finish the picture.

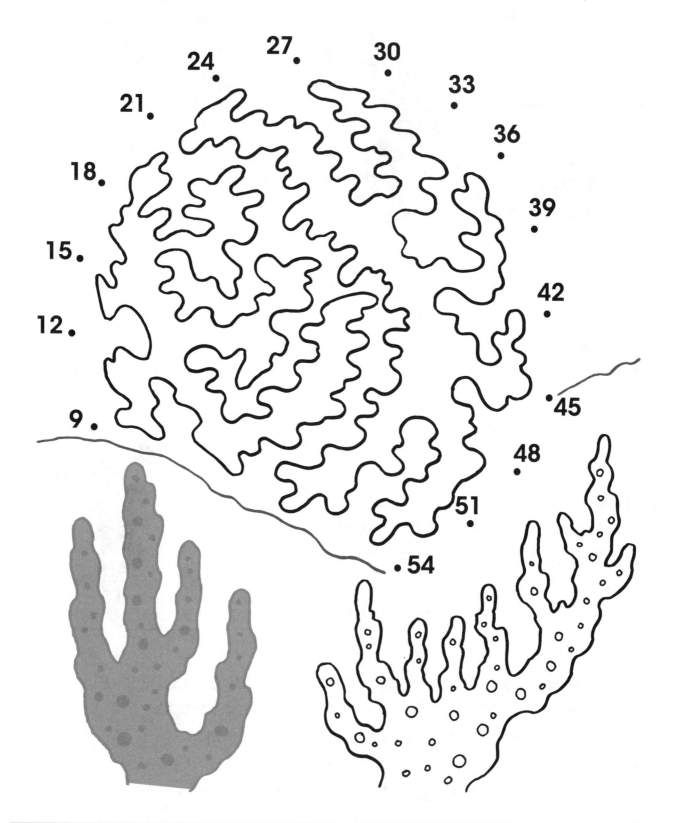

Read All About It

Directions: Read the clues and use the words in the Word Box to complete the puzzle.

Across

2. To send a letter.
5. Not messy.
6. What you are called.
7. A polite word.
8. Pretty.
9. Related to a donkey.
10. A kind of coat you wear around the house.
12. To sparkle.
13. Not shallow.
15. To steer a car.
16. Opposite of **dirty**.

Down

1. Used to catch a fish.
3. Jump.
4. To rob.
5. Friendly and kind.
6. Opposite of **far**.
9. Opposite of **kind**.
11. A dog's treat.
12. To slip.
13. Ten-cent coin.
14. More than one mouse.

deep	mule	dime
cute	slide	name
nice	please	bait
mail	leap	neat
mice	bone	mean
robe	clean	drive
near	steal	shine

An Unsafe Ride

Directions: Help the girl find the helmet.

Career Time

Directions: Use the pictures and words in the Word Box to help you fill in the puzzle.

1.
2.
3.
4.
5.
6.
7.
8.

| doctor |
| teacher |
| artist |
| plumber |
| lawyer |
| singer |
| chef |
| carpenter |

1.  2.  3.  4.

5.  6.  7.  8.

Unscramble Time

Directions: Unscramble each word. Be sure it goes with the meaning.

1. One who plays is called a

   lapeyr __ __ __ __ __ __.

2. A round thing you can kick is a

   lalb __ __ __ __.

3. A sweet treat to eat is

   danyc __ __ __ __ __.

4. Something you can win is a

   pzire __ __ __ __ __.

5. A person who wins is the

   rnnewi __ __ __ __ __ __.

6. One who sails a boat is a

   ailsor __ __ __ __ __ __.

prize
winner
player
ball
sailor
candy

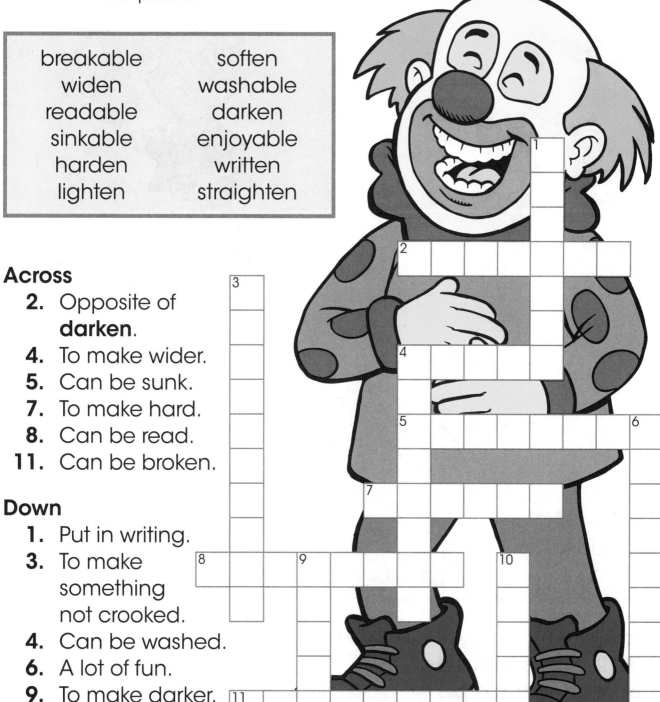

Laughable Fellow

Directions: Read the clues and use the words in the Word Box to complete the puzzle.

breakable	soften
widen	washable
readable	darken
sinkable	enjoyable
harden	written
lighten	straighten

Across

2. Opposite of **darken**.
4. To make wider.
5. Can be sunk.
7. To make hard.
8. Can be read.
11. Can be broken.

Down

1. Put in writing.
3. To make something not crooked.
4. Can be washed.
6. A lot of fun.
9. To make darker.
10. Opposite of **harden**.

An Attack of the Munchies

Directions: Read the clues and use the words in the Word Box to complete the puzzle.

| apple | peanut butter | cheese | carrots |
| cherry | raisin | milk | banana |

Across

3. It comes from cows.
5. It can go in a pie.
7. It is good with jelly.

Down

1. It is brown and sweet.
2. Rabbits like them.
4. It is made from milk.
6. It can be red, yellow, or green.
8. It is yellow and grows in a bunch.

Snow White

Directions: Connect the dots from **25** to **100**. Then, color to finish the picture.

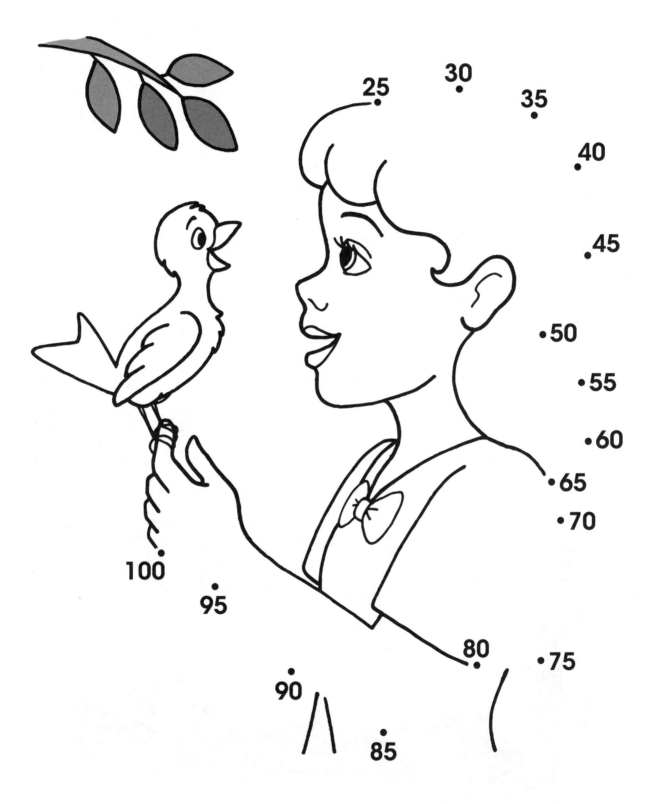

Ticket, Please!

Directions: Find and circle the words in the puzzle.

```
a l m j e f o p q d g u i
c f h i k f f c e b m n p
b e r t y s e v e n z c b
h o e r s j t e n l h n g
u x e t c d o n e t h i k
w f l n y x f e z h d i o
p i e i s t o i e r a u p
d v v n i w u g r e n k l
a e e e x o r h o e d f h
b c n d f g i t j l m n o
```

zero   four   eight
one   five   nine
two   six   ten
three   seven   eleven

TICKET

Favorite Games

Directions: Travel through the maze choosing only games, sports, or things with which you can play.

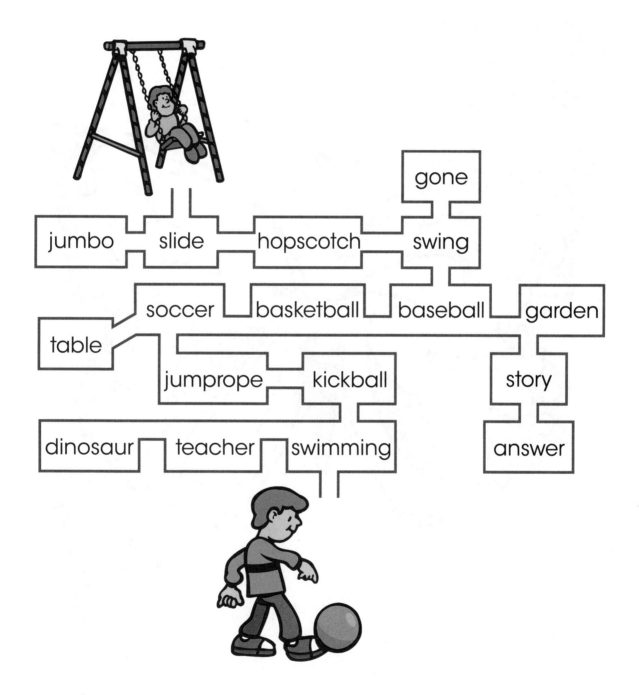

Wet and Dry

Directions: Help the butterflies find the sunshine. Then, color the picture.

Draw a Dinosaur

Directions: These pictures are out of order. Number the steps from **1** to **6**.

Directions: Follow the steps to draw a dinosaur.

Chef Charlie

Directions: Chef Charlie tossed the pizza crust. Where did it go?

Where's Fluffy?

Directions: Help the children find the cat. Then, color the picture.

What Is Happening?

Directions: Circle the names of things in the picture.

fossils	tools	dog
snowman	workers	camera
dirt	hat	money

Directions: Circle and write the best title for the picture.

Hiking in the Desert   Finding Fossils   At the Museum

Nuts, Seeds, and Beans

Directions: Find and circle the words in the puzzle.

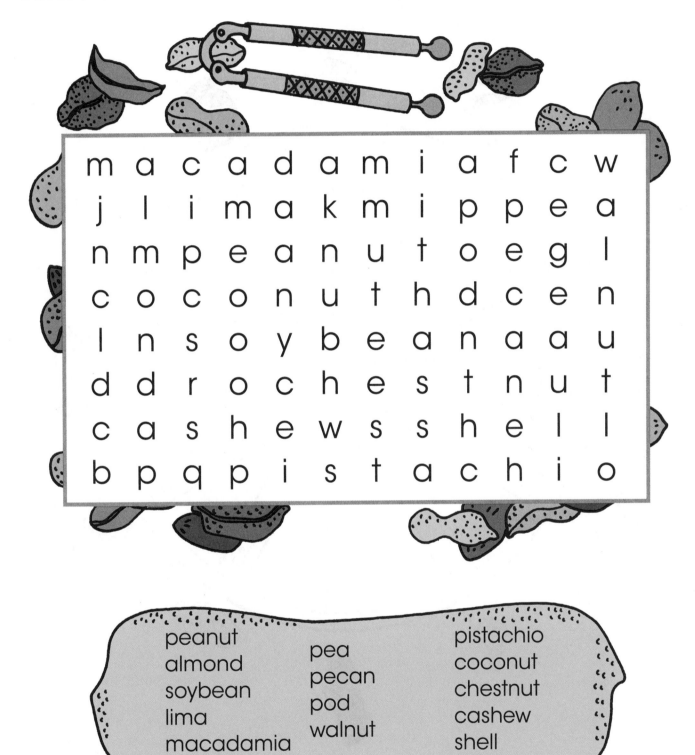

```
m a c a d a m i a f c w
j l i m a k m i p p e a
n m p e a n u t o e g l
c o c o n u t h d c e n
l n s o y b e a n a a u
d d r o c h e s t n u t
c a s h e w s s h e l l
b p q p i s t a c h i o
```

peanut
almond
soybean
lima
macadamia

pea
pecan
pod
walnut

pistachio
coconut
chestnut
cashew
shell

Wagon Wheel

Directions: Write the first letter of the words in the puzzle wheel.

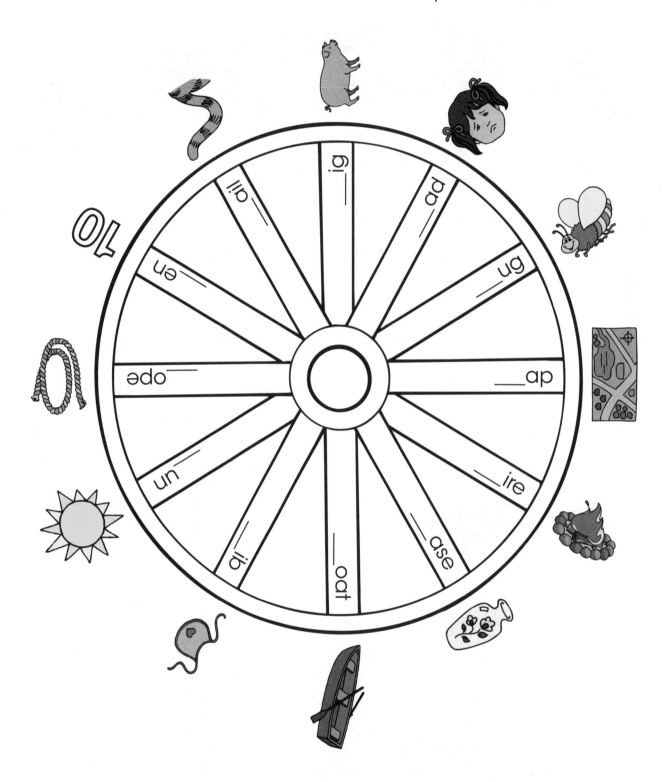

Field Goal

Directions: Kick the football through the goalposts.

Sharpy Swordfish

Directions: Connect the dots from **3** to **27**. Then, color to finish the picture.

Feelings

Directions: Find and circle the words in the puzzle.

```
a h a p p y n s h y j s p
j t n a r q o p m k l u r
e s g v f s o r r y f r o
a b r u w r x s h i g p u
l g y f e y a z a d c r d
o c n d q o p i e d z i y
u h o p e f u l d a b s x
s j i m k l e x c i t e d
h l o v e d v r u s t d w
```

happy	jealous	angry
sad	loved	hopeful
shy	sorry	surprised
excited	proud	afraid

Fun Foods

Directions: Write each word in the correct place.

popcorn	ice cream	lollipop
candy	cookie	cake

1.

2.

3.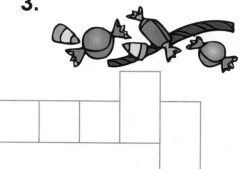

4.

5.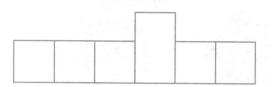

6.

Animal Homes

Directions: Read the clues and use the words in the Word Box to complete the puzzle.

Word Box

web
tree
nest
lodge
hive
hill
shell
pond

Across
3. This is where bees make their honey.
4. This is a home for a clam.
6. Fish and frogs live here.
7. A bird makes this home.

Down
1. Ants build one to live in.
2. This is where a spider lives.
5. A beaver builds a dam near this home.
8. A hole in this makes a good home for a squirrel.

Space Age

Directions: Find and circle the words in the puzzle.

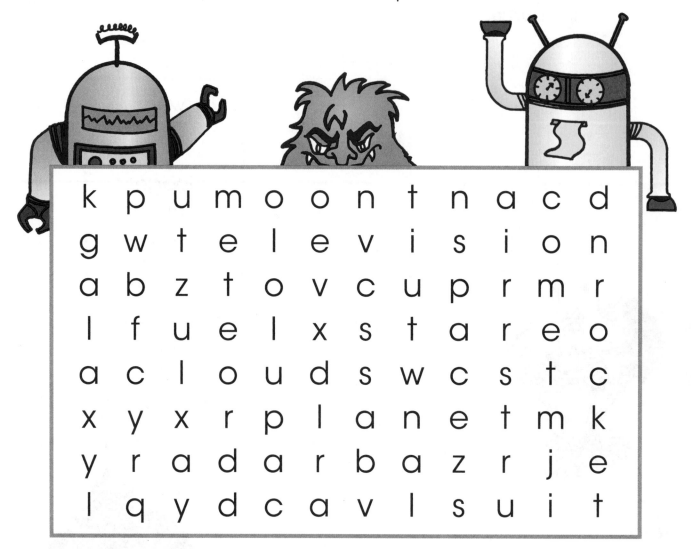

```
k p u m o o n t n a c d
g w t e l e v i s i o n
a b z t o v c u p r m r
l f u e l x s t a r e o
a c l o u d s w c s t c
x y x r p l a n e t m k
y r a d a r b a z r j e
l q y d c a v l s u i t
```

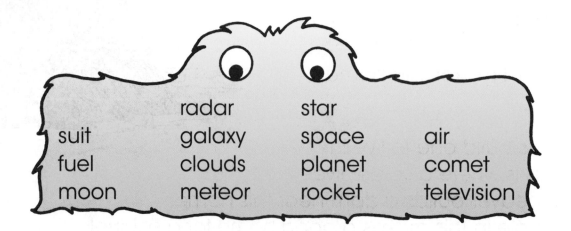

radar   star
suit   galaxy   space   air
fuel   clouds   planet   comet
moon   meteor   rocket   television

I'm Late

Directions: Help the lady get to the train. Then, color the picture.

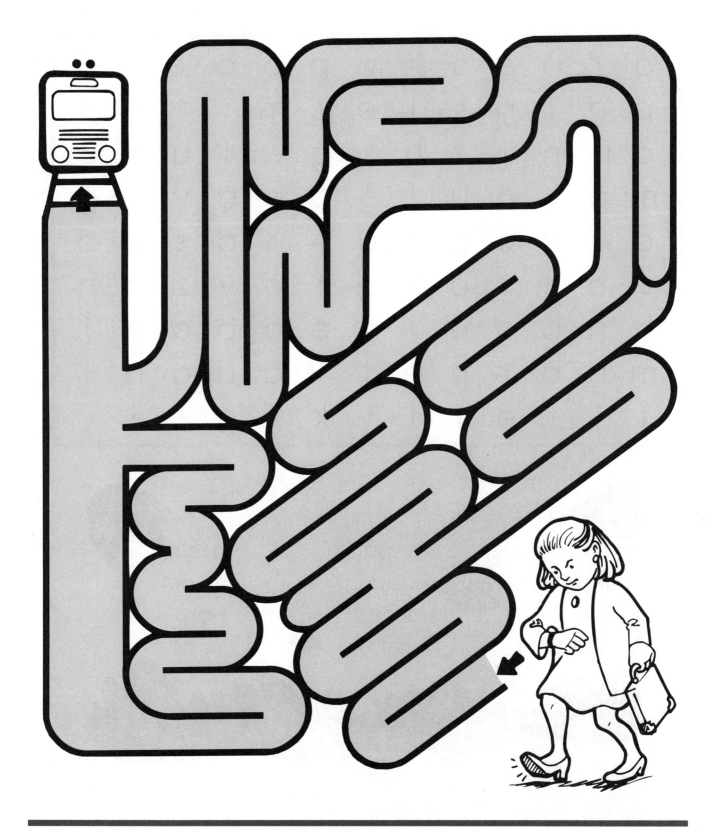

Insects

Directions: Find and circle the words in the puzzle.

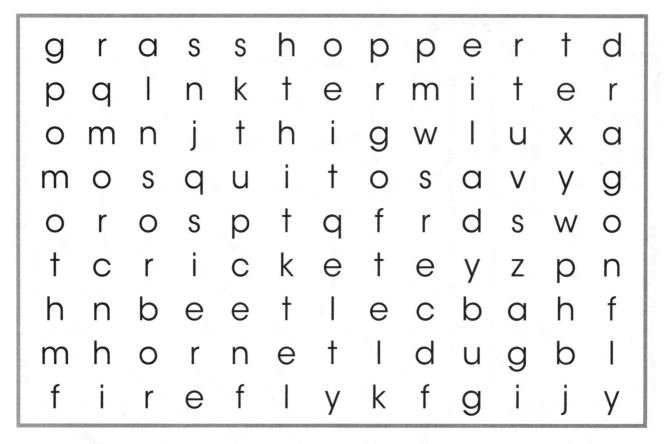

```
g r a s s h o p p e r t d
p q l n k t e r m i t e r
o m n j t h i g w l u x a
m o s q u i t o s a v y g
o r o s p t q f r d s w o
t c r i c k e t e y z p n
h n b e e t l e c b a h f
m h o r n e t l d u g b l
f i r e f l y k f g i j y
```

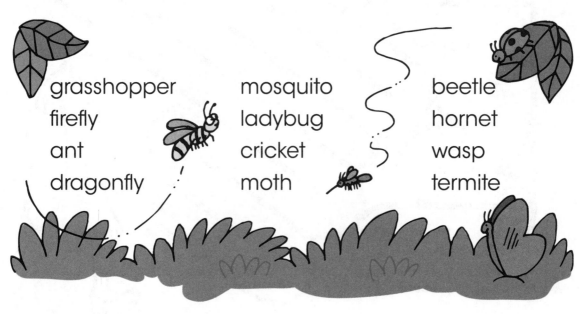

grasshopper   mosquito   beetle

firefly   ladybug   hornet

ant   cricket   wasp

dragonfly   moth   termite

Slumbering Slippers

Directions: Read the clues and use the words in the Word Box to complete the puzzle.

Across

4. Opposite of **frown**.
5. A small, slow-moving creature.
6. Opposite of **rough**.
9. Resting.
10. To slant or lean.
11. What your nose does.
13. Intelligent.
14. Ah . . . choo!

Down

1. To shut with a bang.
2. A smooth, layered rock.
3. A cracking sound.
4. Very clever, like a fox.
6. To trip.
7. A kind of shoe.
8. Reptiles.
11. Frozen white flakes.
12. Something burning gives off.

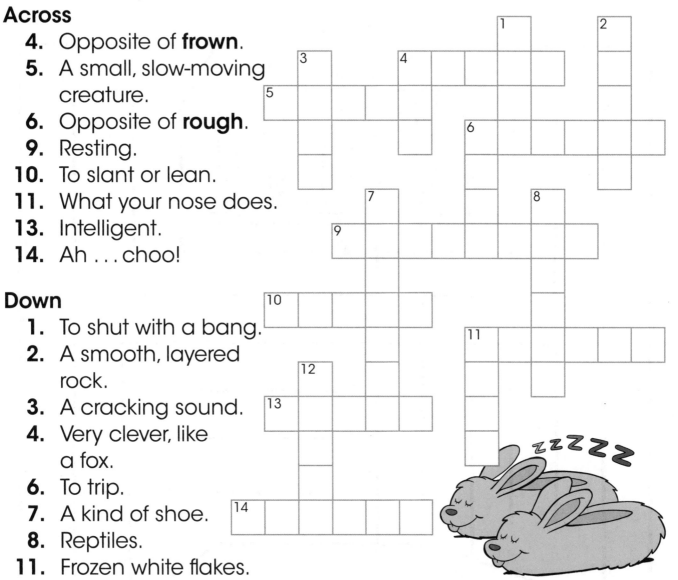

smooth	snail	sly
slam	smart	slip
slipper	snow	smile
slope	slate	smoke
snakes	smells	sneeze
snap	sleeping	

Book Return

Directions: Return the books to the library.

Mystery Picture

Directions: Read each sentence and cross out the picture. What picture is left?

1. It is not a toy.

2. It is not foil.

3. It is not boil.

4. It is not coins.

5. It is not soil.

6. It is not oil.

The mystery picture is a _____ .

Cat and Mouse

Directions: Help the cat find the mouse. Then, color the picture.

One Through Ten

Directions: Find and circle the words in the puzzle.

```
n s o t s o n e f
i i t w o v i m o
n x s e v e n d t
e h e i o b x v h
c t y g m f o u r
u e o h y t p l e
g n b t g f i v e
```

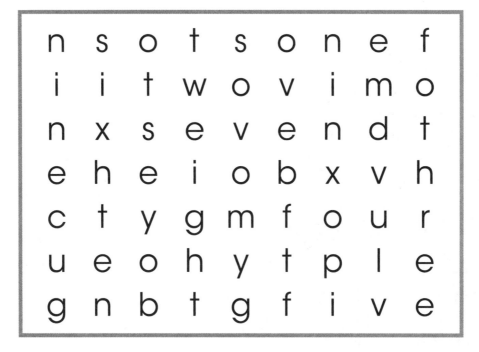

one   six

two   seven

three   eight

four   nine

five   ten

Facing the Sun

Directions: Read the clues and use the words in the Word Box to complete the puzzle.

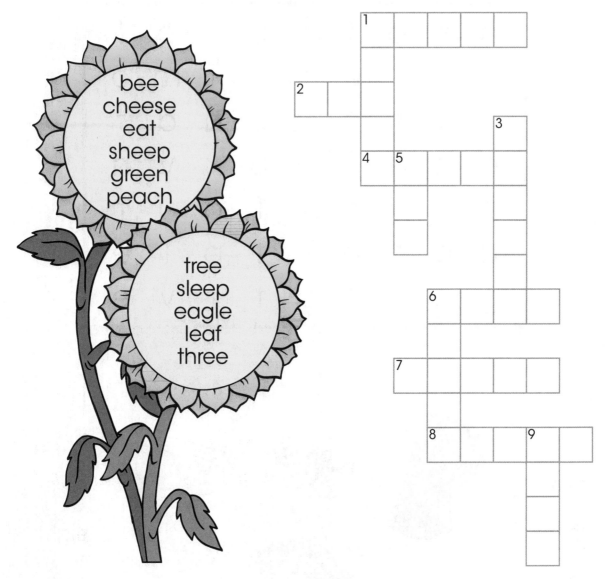

bee
cheese
eat
sheep
green
peach

tree
sleep
eagle
leaf
three

Across

1. A farm animal.
2. A buzzing bug.
4. A fruit.
6. A very tall plant.
7. The color of grass.
8. A big bird.

Down

1. At night you _____.
3. A mouse eats _____.
5. You _____ food.
6. 2 + 1 = _____.
9. A part of a plant.

Ages 7+

Winter

Directions: Read the clues and use the words in the Word Box to complete the puzzle.

snowman
skis
ice
sleep
blizzard
indoors
shovel
bare
sled

Across
1. This is what some animals do in winter.
2. Use this to take the snow off of sidewalks.
3. This is where to stay warm in a snowstorm.
6. It is a snowstorm.

Down
1. You can build one in the snow.
2. Wear two of them on your feet.
4. Ride this down a snowy hill.
5. This is how the trees look in winter.
7. This is water that has frozen.

Rip Van Winkle

Directions: Connect the dots from **4** to **32**. Then, color to finish the picture.

The Elves & the Shoemaker

Directions: Connect the dots from **4** to **56**. Then, color to finish the picture.

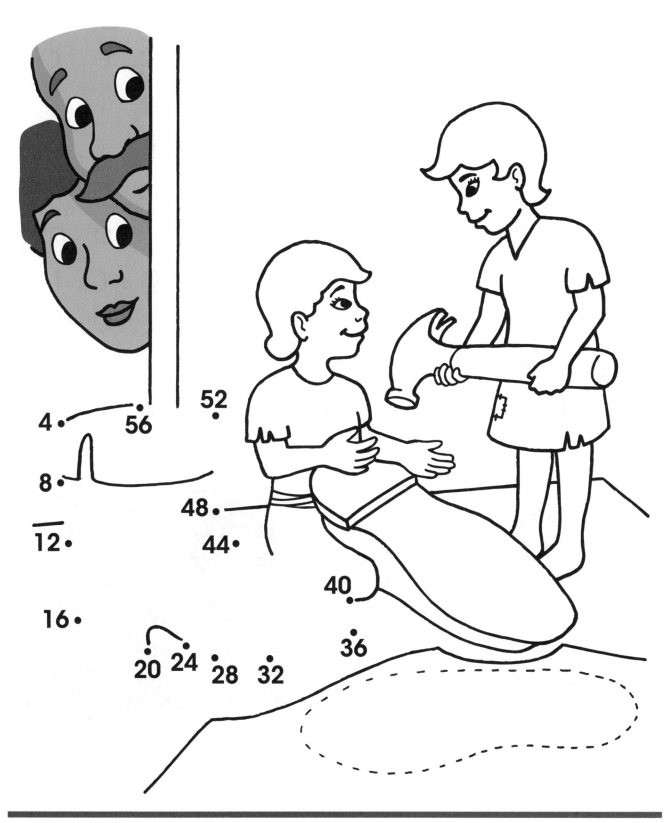

Community Helpers

Directions: Find and circle the words in the puzzle.

```
w  n  u  r  s  e  p  l  u  m  b  e  r
d  x  a  z  y  t  e  a  c  h  e  r  j
o  c  b  c  f  j  a  p  b  l  k  i  d
c  l  d  a  g  h  u  c  m  d  h  b  e
t  e  w  u  k  r  q  d  o  e  i  a  n
o  r  z  v  t  e  s  n  g  f  g  r  t
r  k  b  u  s  d  r  i  v  e  r  b  i
u  m  e  c  h  a  n  i  c  t  s  e  s
f  i  r  e  f  i  g  h  t  e  r  r  t
```

firefighter   clerk
doctor   judge
nurse   mechanic
bus driver   baker
dentist   plumber
teacher   barber

Marty the Mantis

Directions: Connect the dots from **10** to **80**. Then, color to finish the picture.

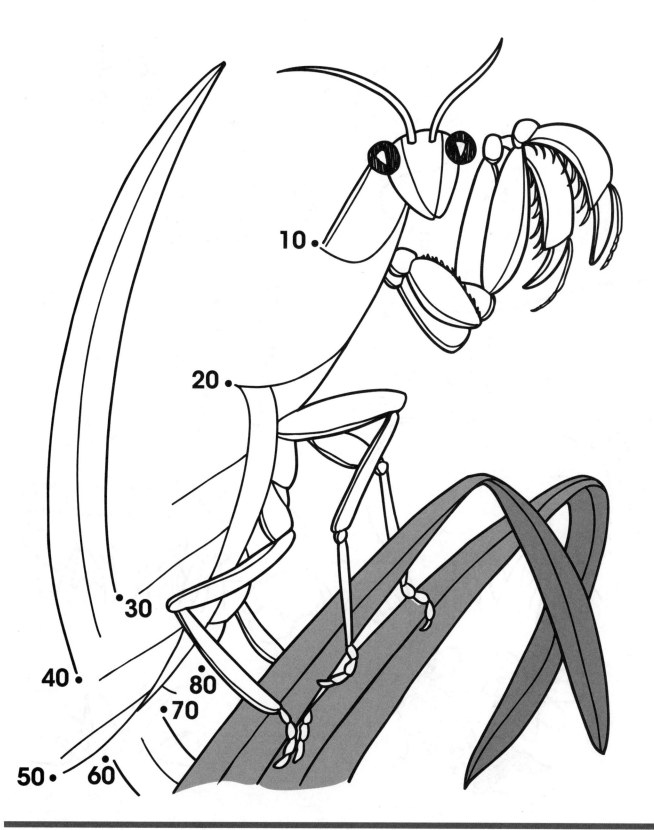

Dana Deer

Directions: Connect the dots from **1** to **15**. Then, color to finish the picture.

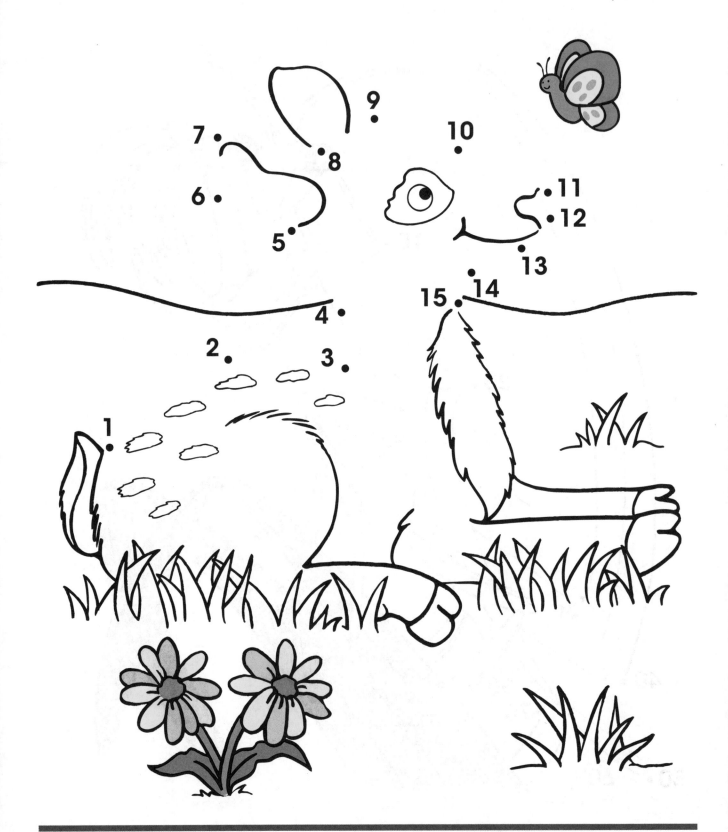

A Hungry Bear

Directions: Help the bear find the honey.

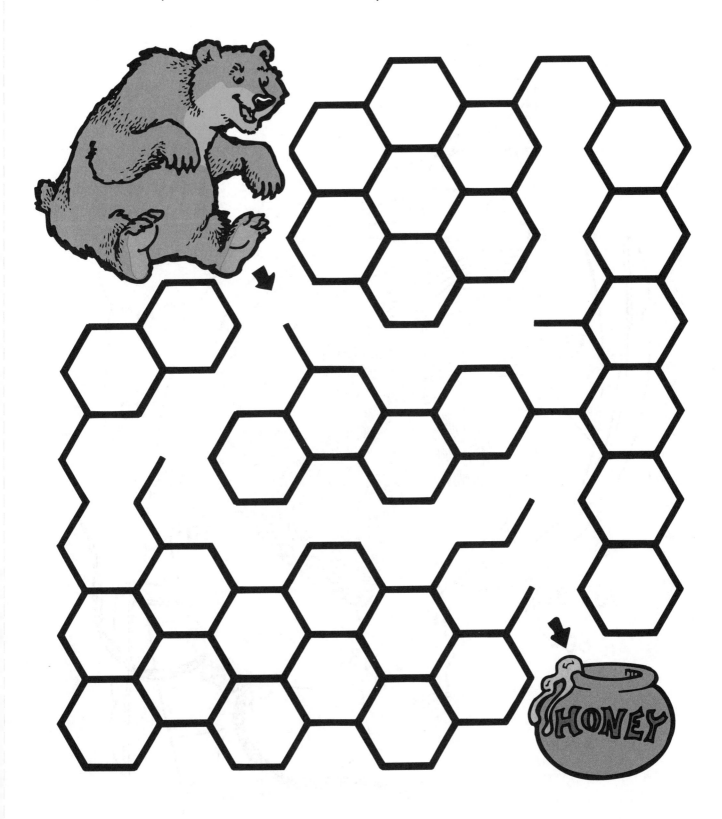

Barry the Beetle

Directions: Connect the dots from **10** to **200**. Then, color to finish the picture.

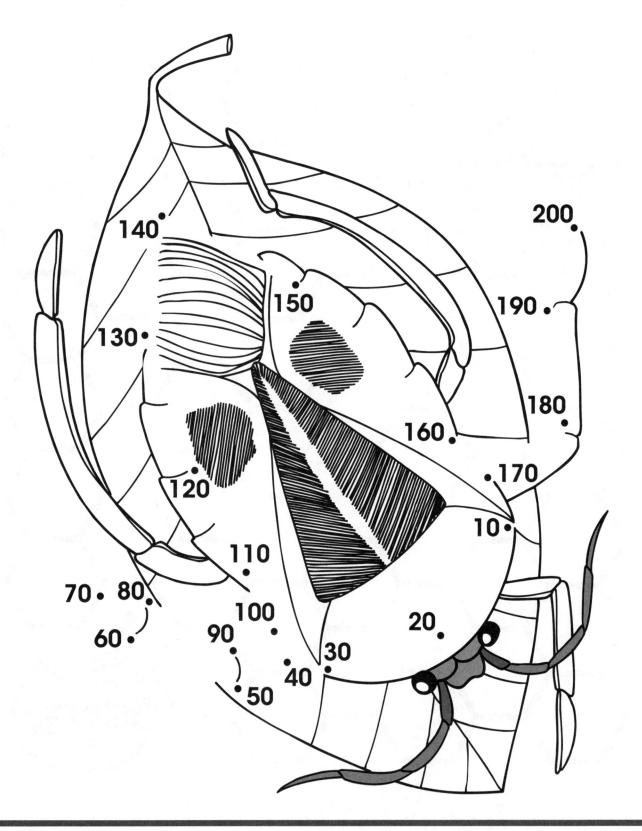

Tools

Directions: Find and circle the words in the puzzle.

```
f  x  d  o  z  h  p  l  e
u  t  r  p  s  a  w  s  k
n  a  i  l  s  m  r  e  c
r  c  l  i  c  m  e  o  p
y  k  l  e  r  e  n  j  d
p  s  c  r  e  r  c  n  m
d  m  n  s  w  p  h  f  e
b  l  p  v  z  e  o  l  s
h  n  j  i  l  t  h  m  o
```

| screw | saw | drill | hammer |
| nails | tacks | wrench | pliers |

The Three Bears

Directions: Connect the dots from **16** to **68**. Then, color to finish the picture.

Humpty Dumpty

Directions: Help Humpty Dumpty find the bandage. Then, color the picture.

Where's the Worm?

Directions: Help the early bird catch the worm.

Instruments

Directions: Find and circle the words in the puzzle.

```
h  r  q  d  r  u  m  k  f  t  u  b  a
s  v  i  o  l  i  n  g  z  r  a  g  b
h  u  j  p  b  h  y  l  e  u  y  u  f
t  a  o  x  n  u  f  m  d  m  c  i  l
i  o  r  g  a  n  g  d  e  p  z  t  u
i  v  j  p  w  s  r  l  a  e  b  a  t
p  i  a  n  o  t  p  c  e  t  v  r  e
m  k  q  n  r  o  u  c  e  l  l  o  w
g  l  s  a  x  o  p  h  o  n  e  x  f
```

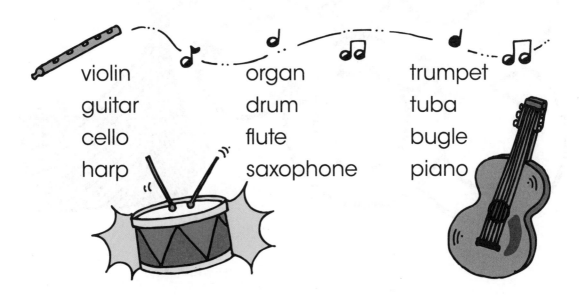

violin   organ   trumpet
guitar   drum   tuba
cello   flute   bugle
harp   saxophone   piano

A Lost Viking

Directions: Help the Viking find his ship.

Shirts and Shoes

Directions: If you put **s** and **h** together, they make the **sh** sound. How many things can you find in this picture that begin with **sh**? Circle them.

shadow
shapes
shark
sheep
shelf
shells
ship
shirt
shoes
shop
shutters

Write three words that begin with **sh**.

_____   _____   _____

Sid Sea Lion

Directions: Connect the dots from **1** to **20**. Then, color to finish the picture.

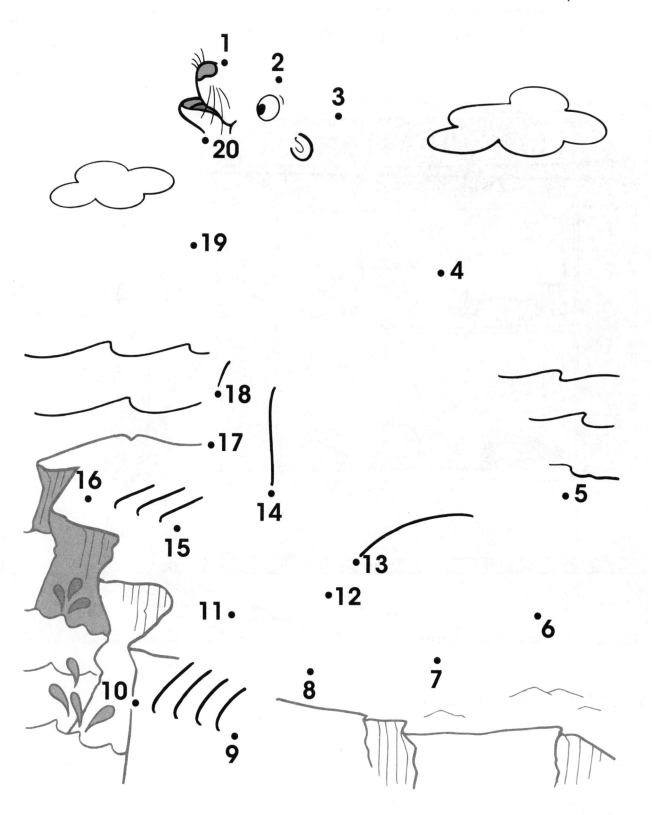

Soldier of the Sea

Directions: Connect the dots from **10** to **28**. Then, color to finish the picture.

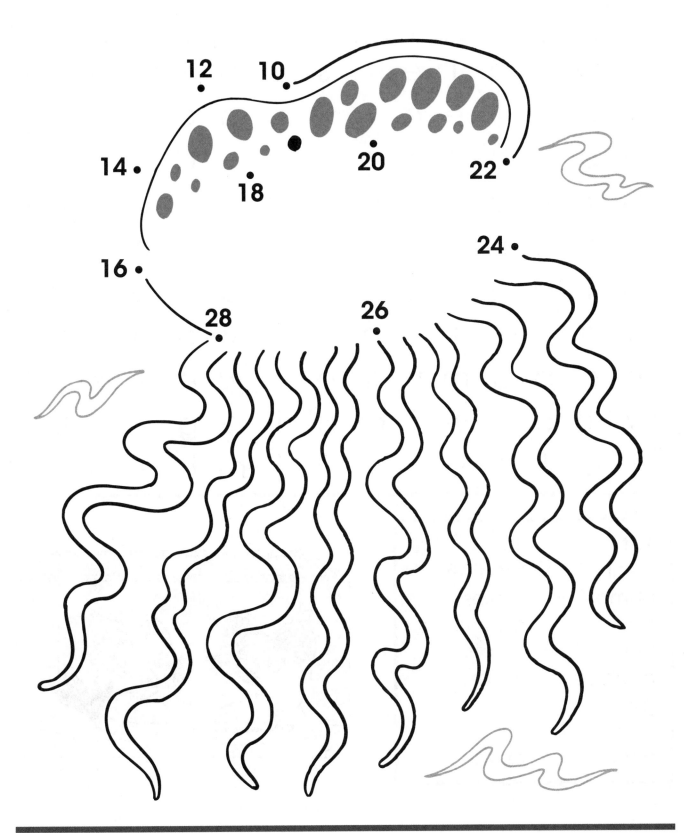

A Refreshing Dip

Directions: Find and circle the words in the puzzle.

```
e  m  w  a  t  e  r  s  i  q  t  a  s  t
t  s  c  l  e  a  r  w  e  a  q  c  j  a
a  b  u  b  b  l  e  s  i  u  a  y  x  c
b  r  e  a  t  h  e  l  a  l  o  p  d  h
r  o  c  k  s  c  a  r  e  f  n  o  e  u
p  l  a  n  t  s  i  s  e  e  i  p  n  m
x  a  i  r  f  u  n  i  l  y  a  n  t  o
b  c  p  u  m  p  s  e  r  w  e  t  s  j
y  i  d  s  w  i  m  u  i  o  g  h  r  k
t  e  f  t  g  i  l  l  j  m  h  i  o  x
```

eat	fins
clear	breathe
pumps	scales
eye	aquariums
fun	plants
bubbles	water
gill	air
swim	tail
care	rocks

Find the Babies

Directions: Find and circle the words in the puzzle.

```
c  u  b  c  z  m  v  t  j  o  e  y  e  d
h  f  l  a  m  b  l  k  p  o  r  e  w  u
i  o  k  l  q  f  p  u  p  o  g  r  e  c
c  a  i  f  d  a  m  k  b  h  y  r  f  k
k  l  d  g  j  w  l  o  e  s  f  l  p  l
k  i  t  t  e  n  o  p  u  y  h  n  v  i
a  w  m  k  i  j  p  l  o  i  y  h  t  n
h  u  y  g  p  i  g  l  e  t  p  m  k  g
```

kid	calf	joey
kitten	cub	pup
chick	foal	duckling
lamb	fawn	piglet

Holidays

Directions: Write the holidays from the Word Box in the puzzle. Then, find the secret word in the heavy boxes going down.

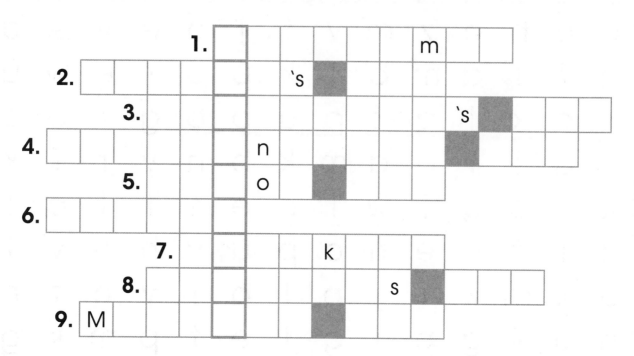

Mother's Day
Father's Day
Veterans Day
Independence Day
Arbor Day
Christmas
Easter
Valentine's Day
Hanukkah

The secret word is _____.

Free to Be Me!

Directions: Connect the dots from **33** to **90**. Then, color to finish the picture.

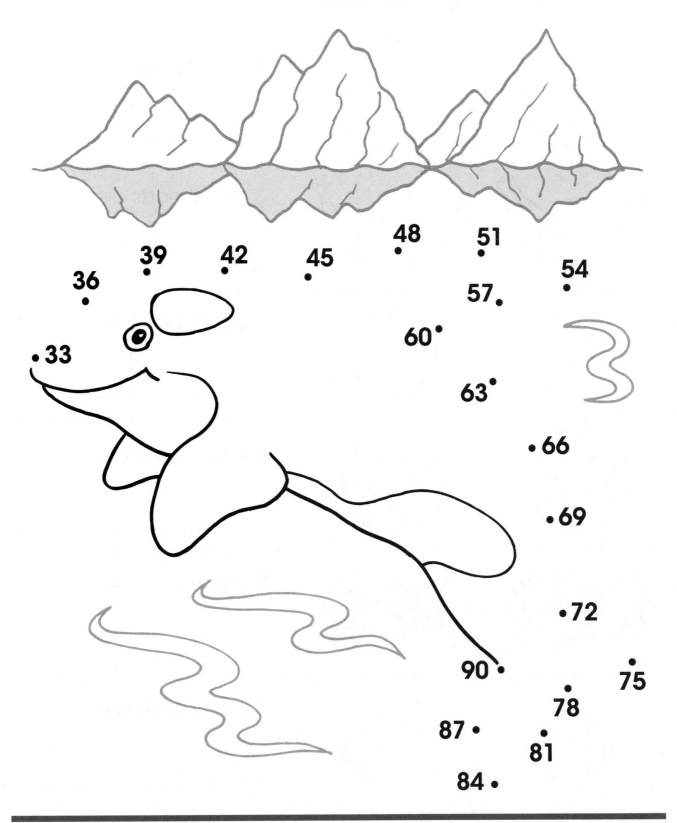

Let's Share It!

Directions: Color the picture in each row that shows equal parts. Then, write the matching fraction word.

  2 equal parts are

halves

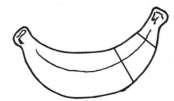 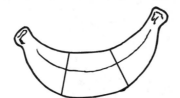 3 equal parts are

thirds

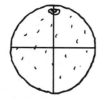  4 equal parts are

fourths

 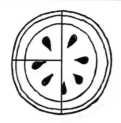 3 equal parts are

_____

  2 equal parts are

_____

4 equal parts are

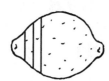 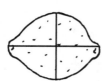

_____

Helpful Friends

Directions: Read the clues and use the words in the Word Box to complete the puzzle.

fireman   alarm
help   careful
accident   obey
matches   siren
policeman

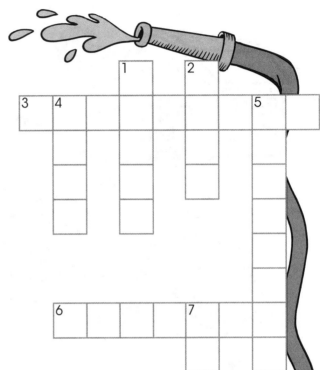

Across

3. A person who works for the police.

6. A person who puts out fires.

9. Always be _____ with fire.

Down

1. Makes a police car's sound.

2. Policemen and firemen _____ everyone.

4. People need to _____ the rules.

5. Police help when there is an _____.

7. Never play with _____.

8. An _____ goes off when there is a fire.

Plump Pig

Directions: Color each **u purple**. Then, color the rest of the picture.

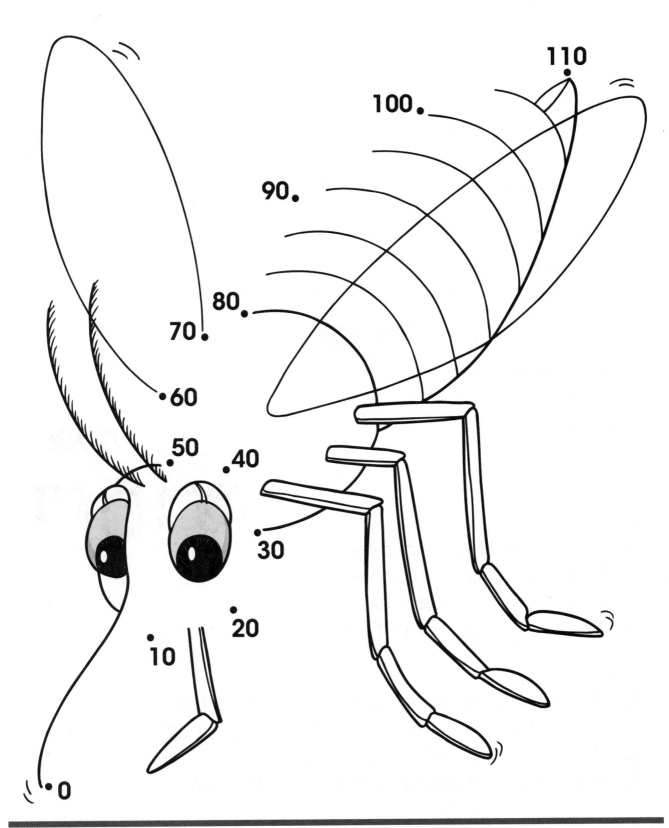

Manny the Mosquito

Directions: Connect the dots from **0** to **110**. Then, color to finish the picture.

Ages 7+

Around the City

Directions: Read the clues and use the words in the Word Box to complete the puzzle.

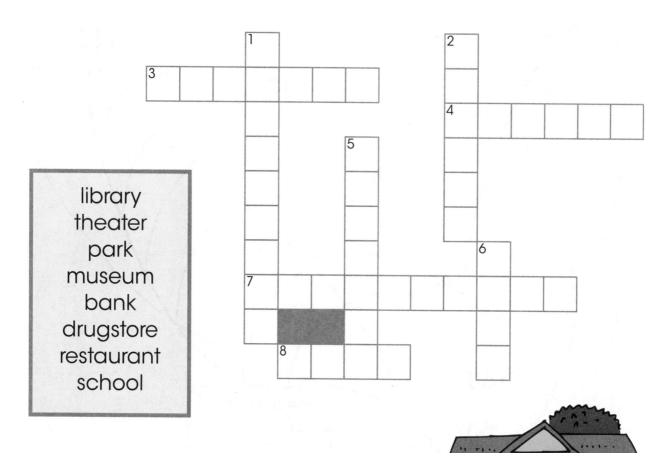

Word Box:
library
theater
park
museum
bank
drugstore
restaurant
school

Across
3. You can borrow books here.
4. Teachers help children learn here.
7. You can get something to eat here.
8. This is where you can go to play or ride a bike.

Down
1. Your mother or father can get medicine here.
2. This building has things about science, antiques, or art.
5. This is where you can see a movie.
6. This is a place where people keep money.

Aladdin & the Lamp

Directions: Connect the dots from **4** to **40**. Then, color to finish the picture.

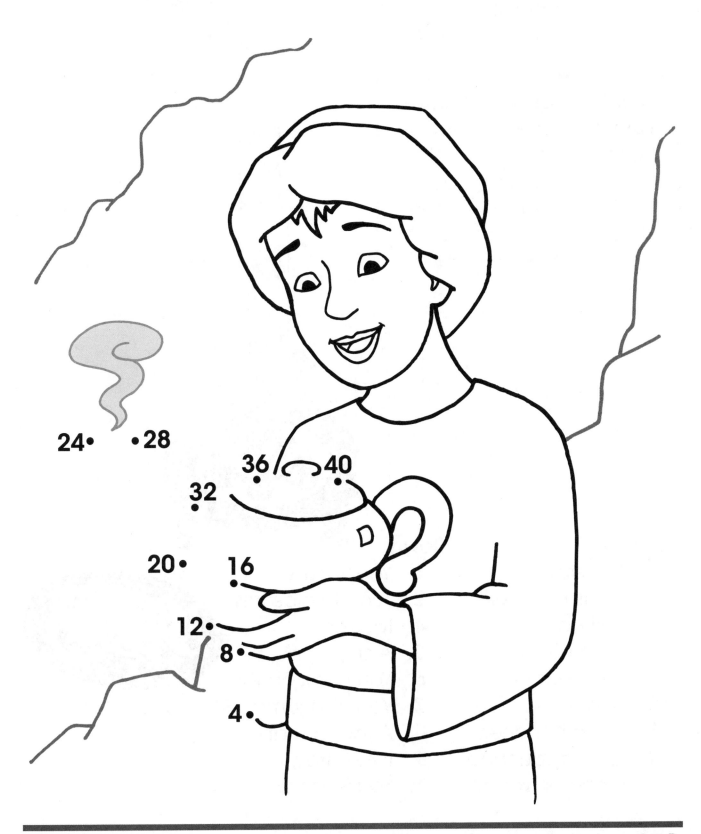

24• •28

36 •40
32

20• •16

12•
8•

4•

Soooo . . . Cozy

Directions: Read the clues and use the words in the Word Box to complete the puzzle.

stone	open	home
bones	toes	road
doe	hole	notes
rope	soap	boat
pole	globe	stove
toad		

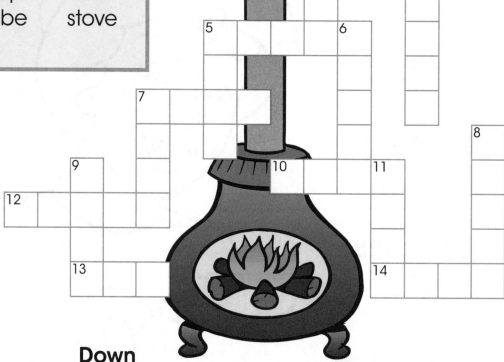

Across

3. Not shut.
5. Dogs like these.
7. A street.
10. These are on your feet.
12. A rock.
13. A mother deer.
14. A long, rounded piece of wood.

Down

1. Your house.
2. A mole digs this.
4. Musical.
5. A ship.
6. You cook on this.
7. You can jump with this.
8. A round map.
9. Like a frog.
11. You wash with this.

Thumbelina

Directions: Connect the dots from **0** to **30**. Then, color to finish the picture.

A Tiger Shell?

Directions: Connect the dots from **26** to **60**. Then, color to finish the picture.

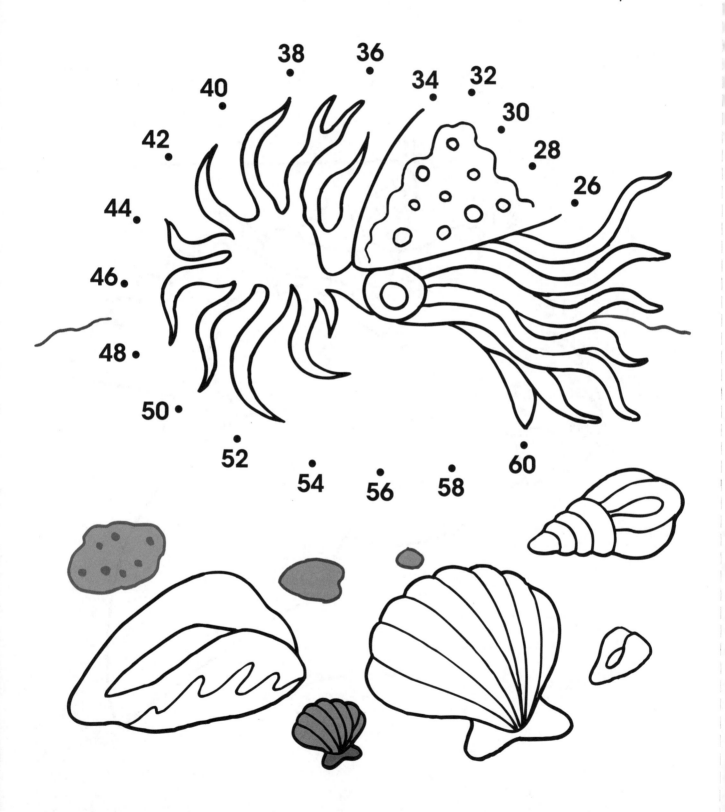

Dinosaur Stories

Directions: Read the book titles. Color story books **red**. Color fact books **blue**.

Digging Up Fossils

Dinosaurs Go to the Moon

All About Dinosaurs

The Kid Who Lived With Dinosaurs

When Dinosaurs Lived on Earth

Jesse Rides a Dinosaur

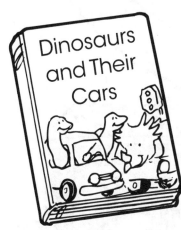

Dinosaurs and Their Cars

Dilbert Dinosaur Goes to School

Why the Dinosaurs Died

Time to Clean Up

Directions: Take the toys to the toy box.

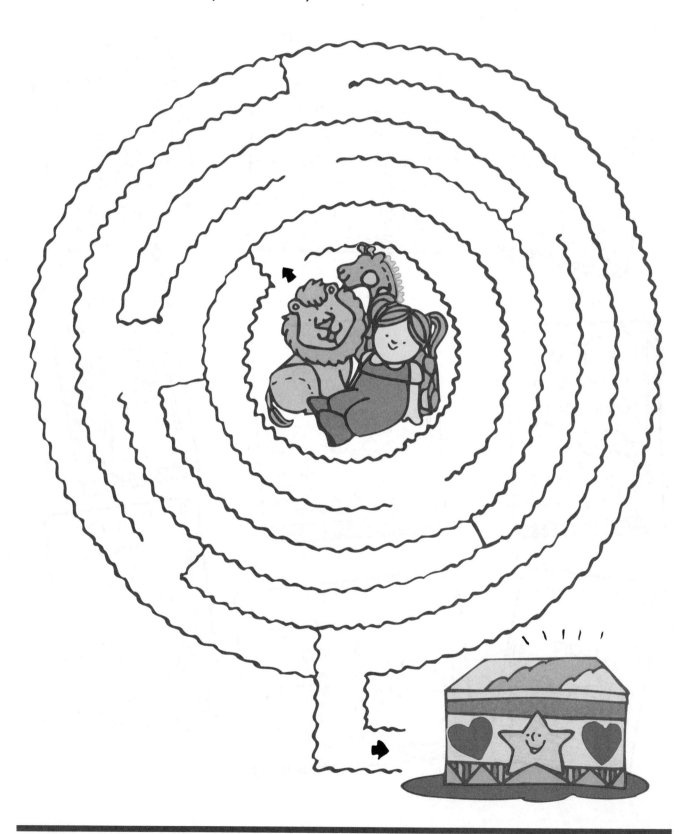

Bicycles

Directions: Find and circle the words in the puzzle.

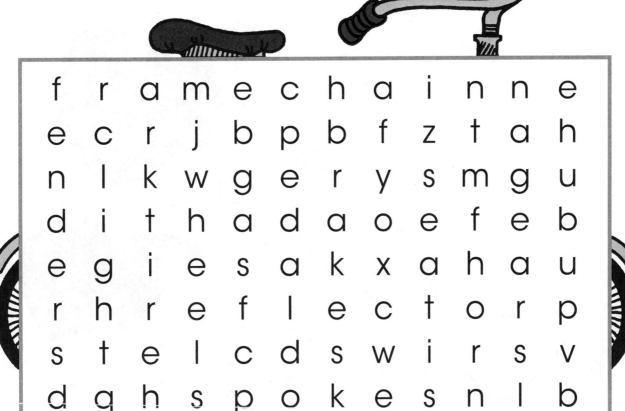

```
f  r  a  m  e  c  h  a  i  n  n  e
e  c  r  j  b  p  b  f  z  t  a  h
n  l  k  w  g  e  r  y  s  m  g  u
d  i  t  h  a  d  a  o  e  f  e  b
e  g  i  e  s  a  k  x  a  h  a  u
r  h  r  e  f  l  e  c  t  o  r  p
s  t  e  l  c  d  s  w  i  r  s  v
d  q  h  s  p  o  k  e  s  n  l  b
```

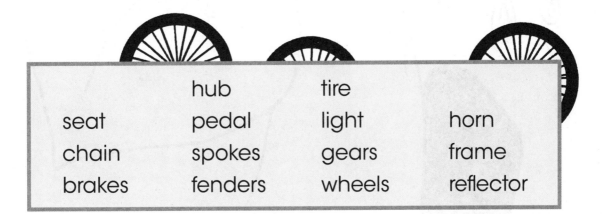

	hub	tire	
seat	pedal	light	horn
chain	spokes	gears	frame
brakes	fenders	wheels	reflector

Jack & the Beanstalk

Directions: Connect the dots from **5** to **60**. Then, color to finish the picture.

Buddy the Bee

Directions: Connect the dots from **0** to **60**. Then, color to finish the picture.

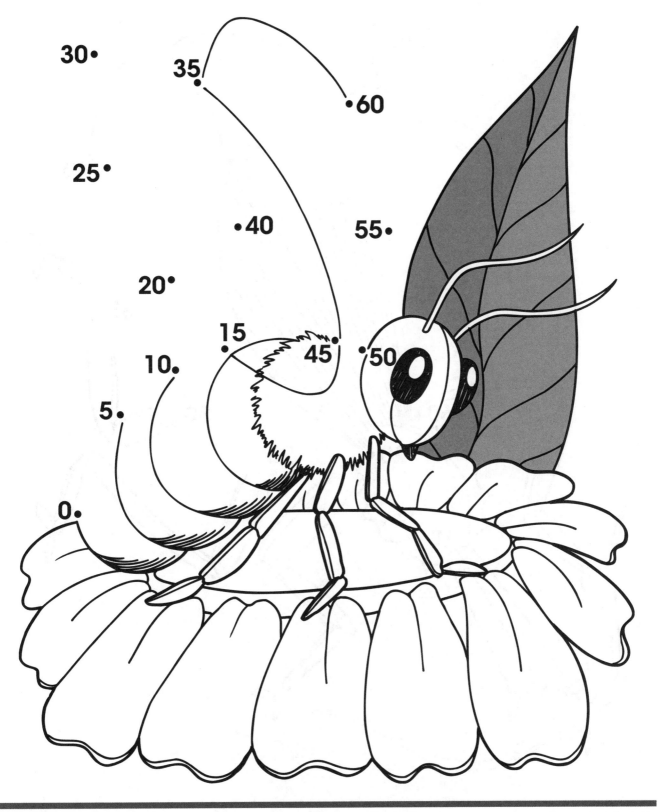

Violet the Violin Beetle

Directions: Connect the dots from **10** to **75**. Then, color to finish the picture.

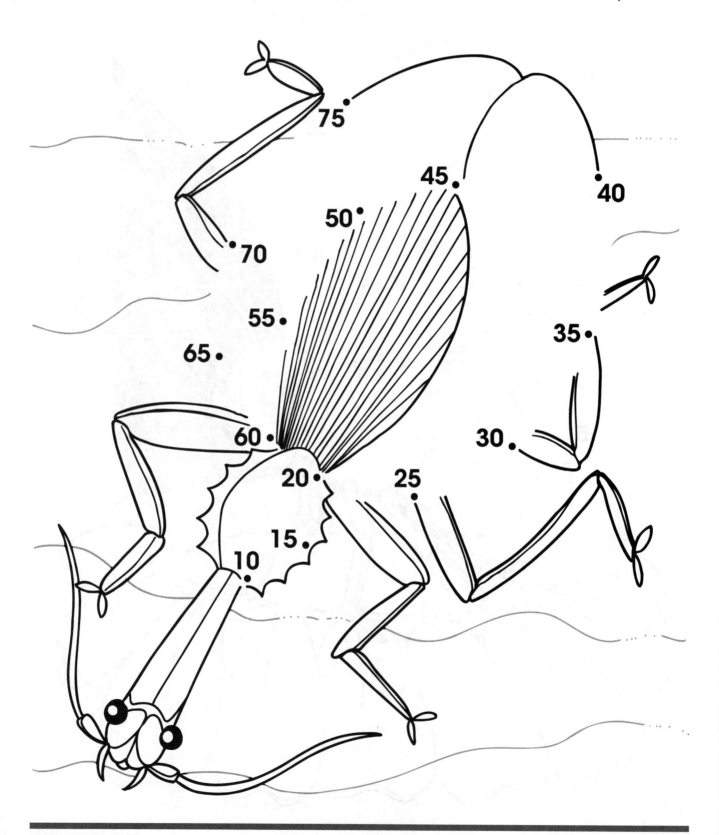

Fly Away

Directions: Find the path back to the town.

The Genie

Directions: Connect the dots from **8** to **36**. Then, color to finish the picture.

A Bumpy Ride

Directions: Help the cowboy reach the town.

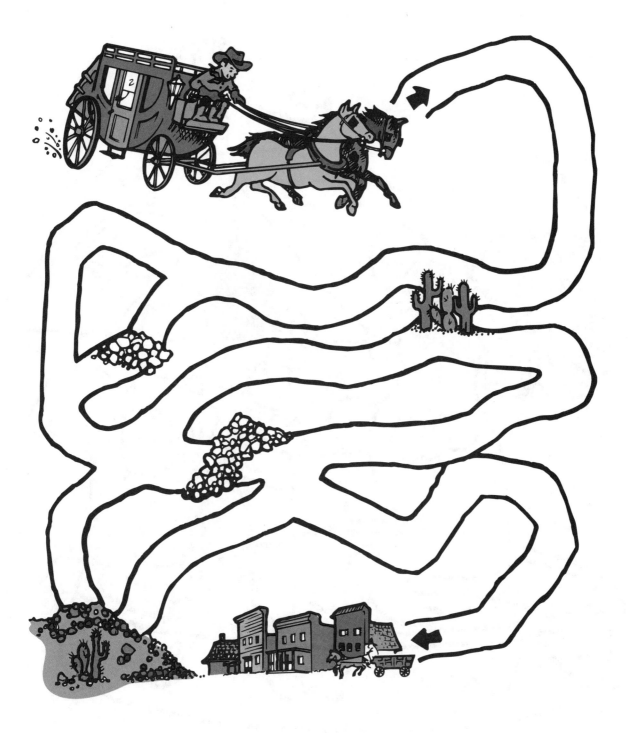

Super Circus

Directions: Color each **v** green. Then, color the rest of the picture.

At School

Directions: Read the clues and use the words in the Word Box to complete the puzzle.

Word Box:
teacher
children
books
computer
desk
read
write
learn

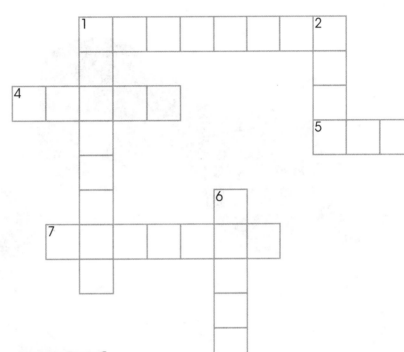

Across
1. This is a machine that helps you learn.
4. You do this with a pencil or a computer.
5. This is where you can work in school.
7. This is a person who helps you learn.

Down
1. These are young people who go to school.
2. This is what you do with a book.
3. These have words and pictures in them.
6. This means **to find out about things**.

A Plate of Spaghetti

Directions: Take the fork to the bottom of the plate of pasta.

Summer

Directions: Read the clues and use the words in the Word Box to complete the puzzle.

green
birds
butterflies
bees
hot
sunny
swim
picnic

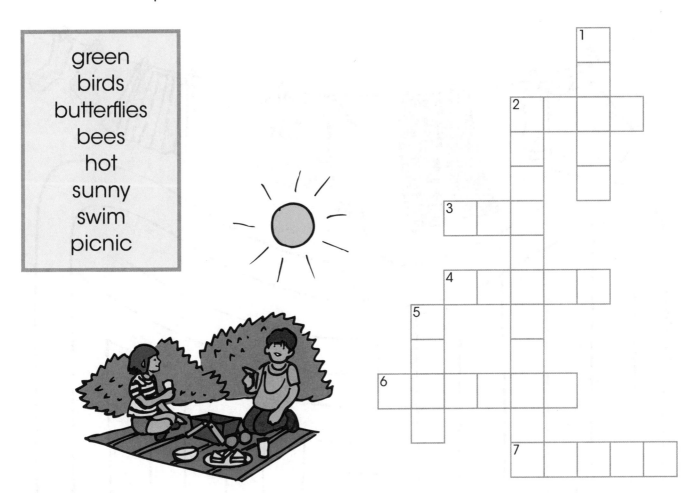

Across
2. These buzz around flowers.
3. It is the opposite of **cold**.
4. You might hear them chirp and sing.
6. Bring your lunch outside for this.
7. This kind of day is good for playing outside.

Down
1. Leaves and grass are this color.
2. They flutter their colorful wings.
5. This feels good to do on a hot summer day.

All Dry

Directions: The clothes are dry. Help put them in the basket.

Let's Play

Directions: Use the words in the Word Box to help you write the name of each picture.

1.

| | | l | |

2.

| | i | | |

3.

| s | | | | s |

4.

| | | g | |

5.

| g | | | |

6.

| | w | n | |

7.

| | r | | |

8.

| | | | m |

Word Box:

bike

skates

ball

swing

wagon

truck

swim

game

Patty Panda

Directions: Connect the dots from **1** to **30**. Then, color to finish the picture.

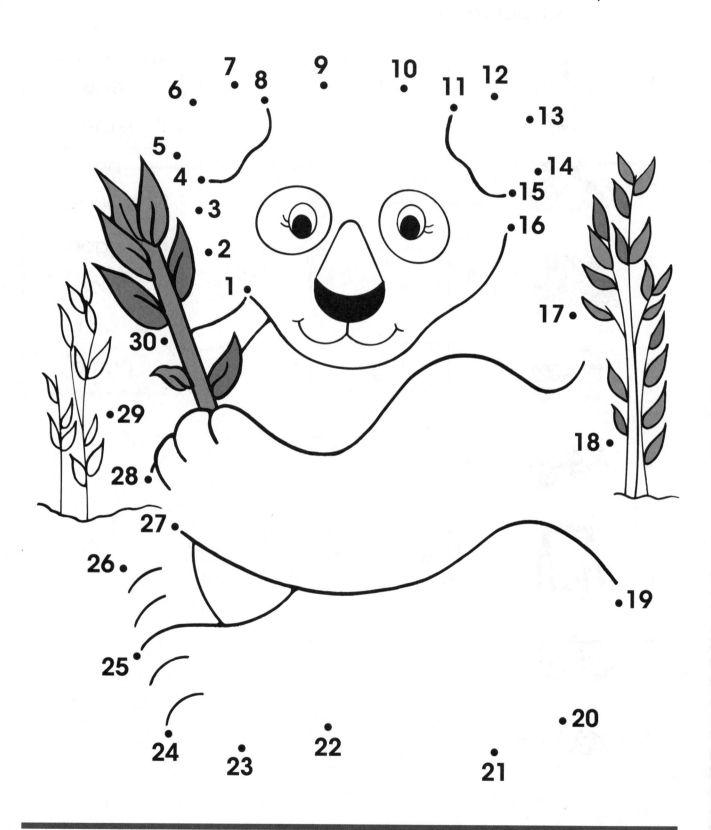

Time to Rhyme

Directions: Use the picture clues to match the rhyming words.

1.  meat

2. seal

3. king

4. mouse

5. clock

6. hair

7. dog

8. boat

 sock

 wheel

 bear

 ring

 goat

 frog

 feet

 house

Fall

Directions: Read the clues and use the words in the Word Box to complete the puzzle.

leaves
pumpkin
apples
moon
yellow
squirrels
geese
rake

Across
3. They gather nuts.
5. Use this to gather fallen leaves.
6. These change color in the fall.
8. This looks big and bright in the sky.

Down
1. Pick a big, orange one.
2. They fly south in the fall.
4. Leaves turn red, brown, and this color.
7. Pick a basket of red, ripe ones.

In Space

Directions: Help the astronaut find the radio. Then, color the picture.

Amy the Atlas Moth

Directions: Connect the dots from **0** to **60**. Then, color to finish the picture.

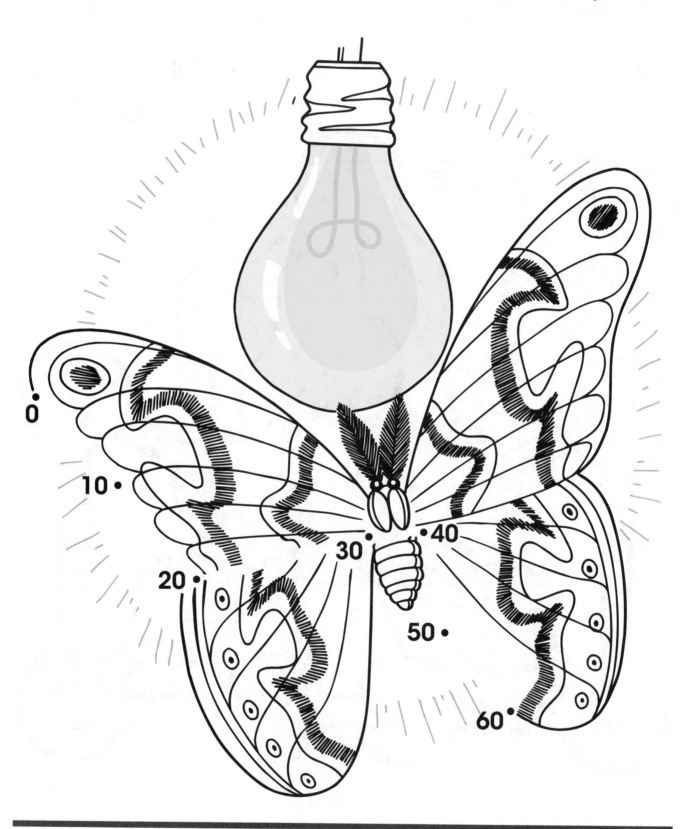

0
10
20
30
40
50
60

For the Birds

Directions: Write the bird names from the Word Box in the puzzle.

1. | | a | |
2. | | | |
3. | | g | |
4. | | |
5. | | | | t | |
6. | o | | | | |
7. | | e | | | |
8. | b | | | | |

buzzard   ostrich   eagle

jay   robin   owl

pigeons   parrots

A Last Dinosaur

Directions: Connect the dots from **28** to **96**. Then, color to finish the picture.

Katie the Katydid

Directions: Connect the dots from **10** to **120**. Then, color to finish the picture.

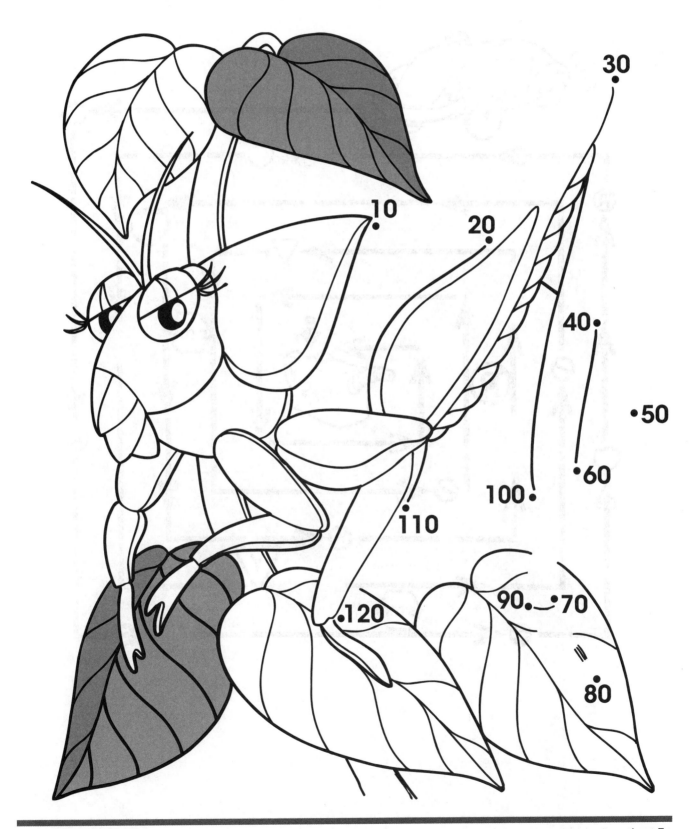

Ages 7+

Out of Gas

Directions: Help the car get to the gas. Then, color the picture.

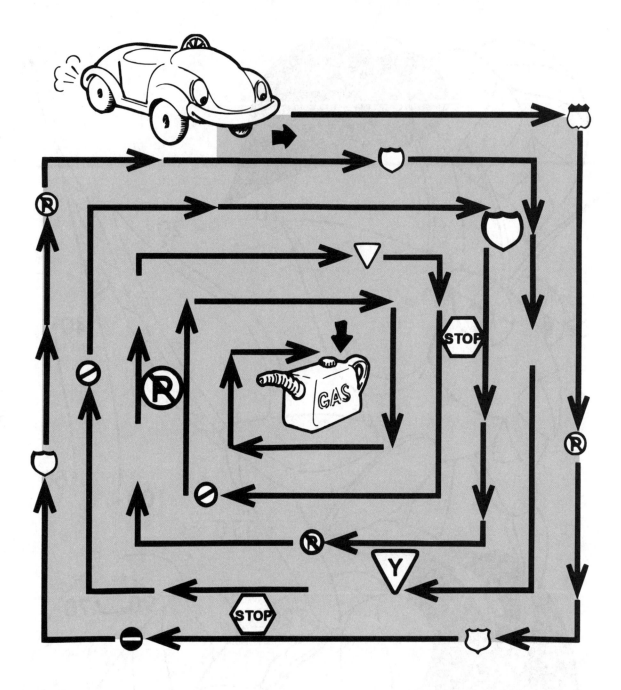

The Little Mermaid

Directions: Connect the dots from **5** to **40**. Then, color to finish the picture.

5•

35

40

10•

•30

•25

15•

•20

The Calendar

Directions: Read the clues and use the words in the Word Box to complete the puzzle.

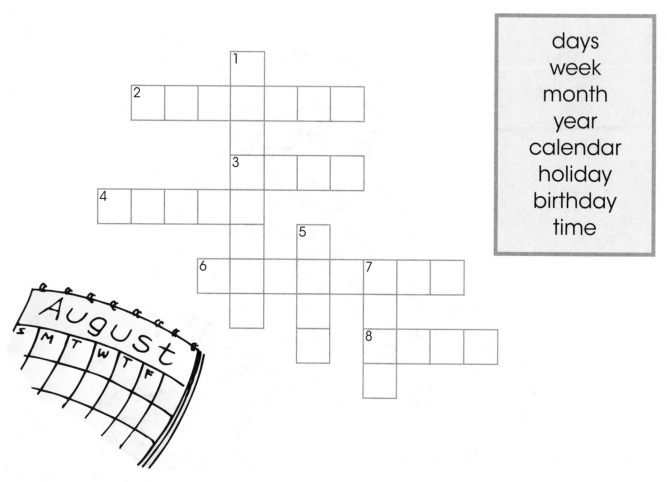

Word Box:
days
week
month
year
calendar
holiday
birthday
time

Across

2. It is a day for celebrating instead of working.
3. It can be measured in days, weeks, months, and years.
4. It can have 28 to 31 days.
6. You can hang it on a wall to keep track of the days.
8. This has twelve months.

Down

1. This is the day you were born.
5. It has seven days.
7. A year has 365 of these.

Camping

Directions: Find and circle the words in the puzzle.

```
g b i b s t e n t j r d
s o f f l s k e j u t c
t o i o a w s l a s e a
o t r o p e q x c w c m
v s e d p a c k k y l e
e h u m a t c h e s o r
h f w a t e r b t p t a
e i n p d r c o a z h c
```

map
tent
rope

stove
water
jacket
camera

fire
food
sweater
matches

pack
boots
cloth

The Emperor's New Clothes

Directions: Connect the dots from **12** to **48**. Then, color to finish the picture.

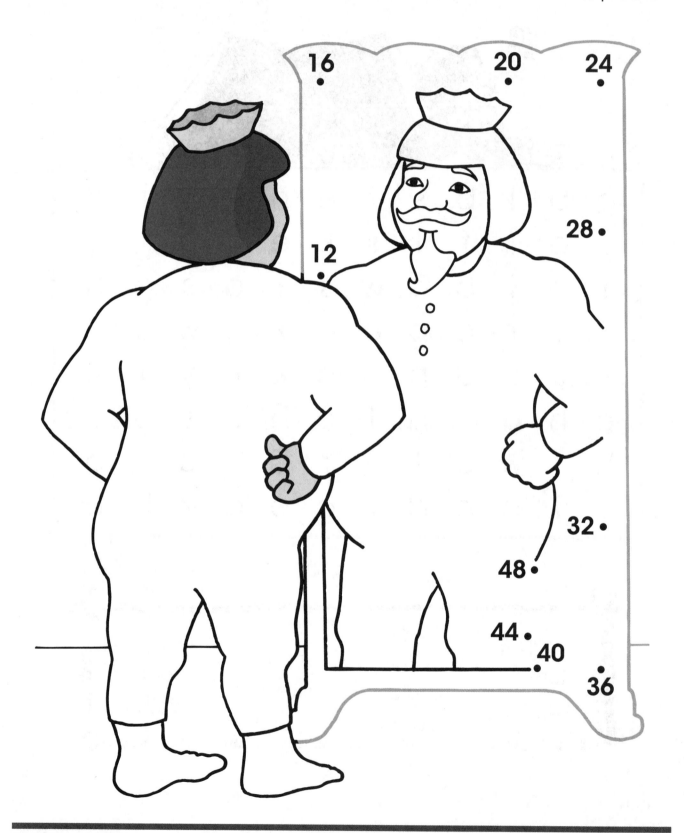

Way to Go!

Directions: Find and circle the words in the puzzle.

```
s g a b g t h o v i w a k l o h
f t r u c k e l e v a t o r n e
s s h i p e s c a l a t o r b c
u b o a t c a b l e c a r s h w
p t a x i s c h o o l b u s e g
x t r a i n s a i r p l a n e v
o t r a m h e l i c o p t e r a
f s u b w a y m o n o r a i l n
n o s b u s o e f a c a b t p s
y n e c a r u n f t j e t o i e
```

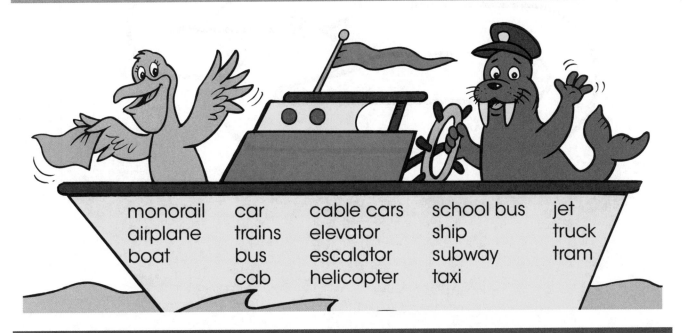

monorail	car	cable cars	school bus	jet
airplane	trains	elevator	ship	truck
boat	bus	escalator	subway	tram
	cab	helicopter	taxi	

A Lost Bead

Directions: Find the path to the missing bead.

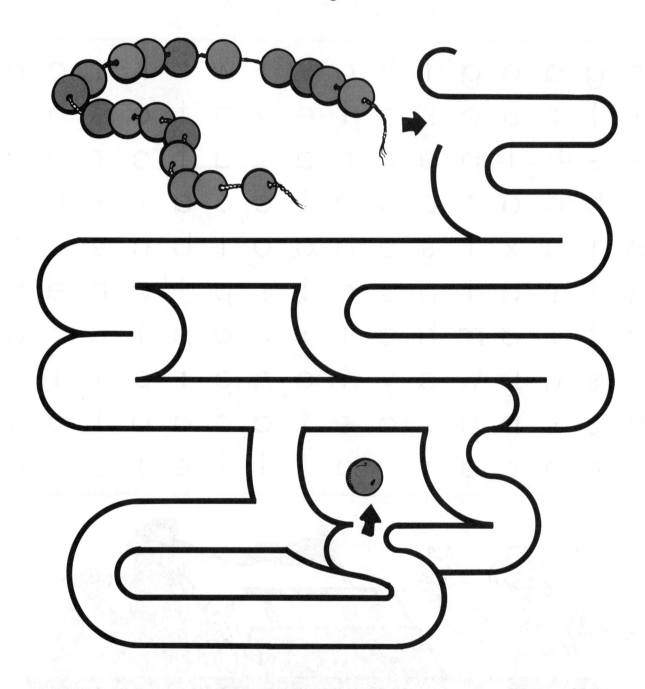

Around the World

Directions: Read the clues and use the words in the Word Box to complete the puzzle.

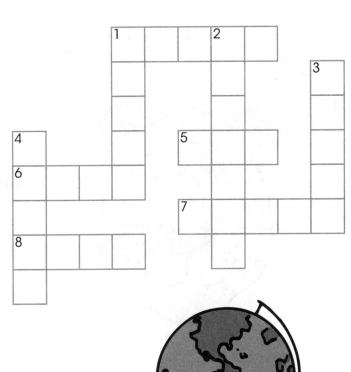

Word Box

map
north
south
globe
water
land
ball
equator
world

Across

1. It is blue on a globe.
5. It is a drawing of land and water on Earth.
6. It is green on a globe.
7. The direction moving toward the bottom of the globe.
8. A globe is shaped like a ____.

Down

1. A globe is a map of this.
2. It is an imaginary line around the middle of Earth.
3. The direction moving toward the top of the globe.
4. It is a model of Earth that is shaped like a ball.

Larry Lion

Directions: Connect the dots from **1** to **25**. Then, color to finish the picture.

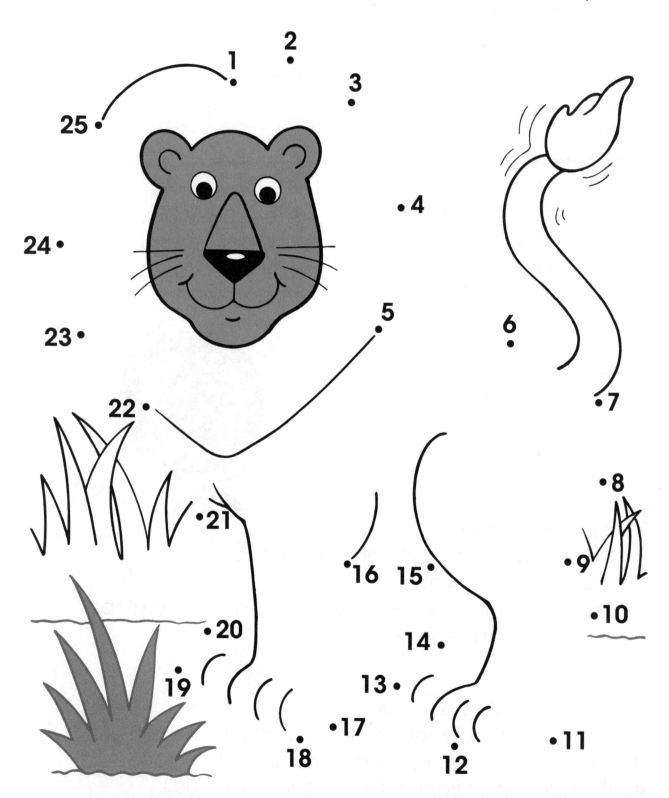

Hot or Cold?

Directions: Draw straight lines to connect the words that name hot or cold things.

ant	ball	snow
sun	ice	fire
snowman	book	ice cream

How many ways did you draw a line through three words in a row? _____

The Giant

Directions: Connect the dots from **10** to **65**. Then, color to finish the picture.

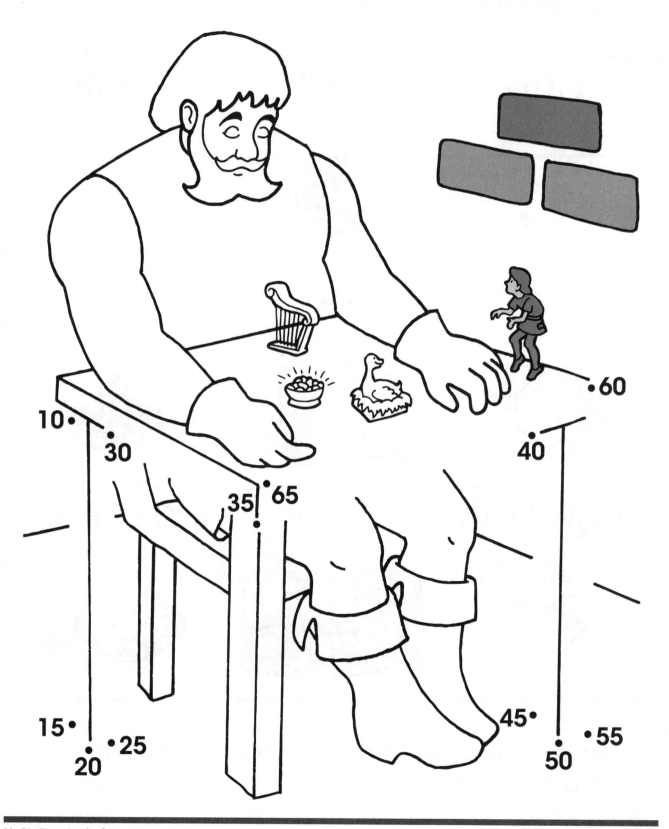

Grammar

Directions: Find and circle the words in the puzzle.

c	a	p	i	t	a	l	v	w	m	q	k
b	d	h	l	v	e	r	b	n	o	u	i
d	v	j	n	r	t	q	u	o	t	e	s
s	e	n	t	e	n	c	e	u	q	s	g
p	r	o	n	o	u	n	u	n	s	t	e
f	b	p	s	u	b	j	e	c	t	i	c
p	h	r	a	s	e	p	e	r	i	o	d
e	x	c	l	a	m	a	t	i	o	n	a

noun	phrase	capital
pronoun	sentence	exclamation
subject	verb	quotes
adverb	period	question

Fun in Art Class

Directions: Read the clues and use the words in the Word Box to complete the puzzle.

paintbrush
color
paper
clay
glue
paints
chalk
scissors
markers

Across

2. Use this to make paper stick together.
5. Remember to put the caps back on these.
7. Make a pot with this.
8. Use your brushes with these.
9. Draw a picture on this.

Down

1. Purple is one.
3. Use this to spread paint on paper.
4. Make sidewalk drawings with this.
6. Use this to cut scraps for a picture.

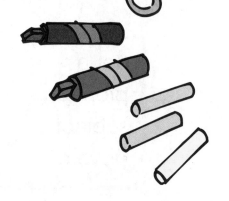

A Lost Kangaroo

Directions: Help the mother kangaroo find her baby.

Buildings and Homes

Directions: Find and circle the words in the puzzle.

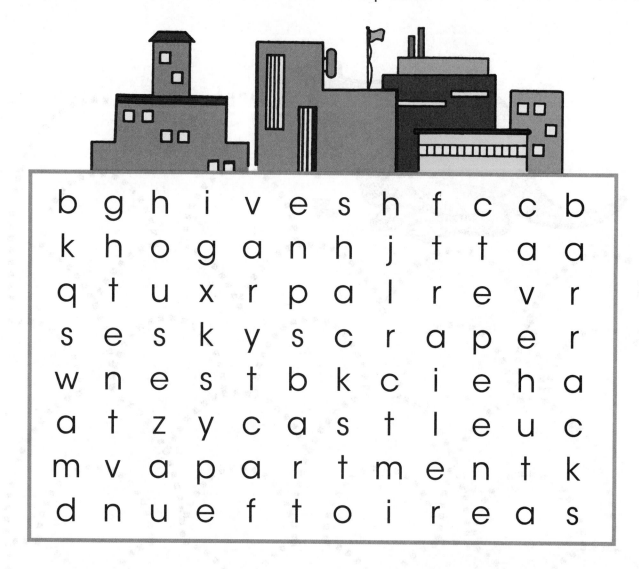

b g h i v e s h f c c b
k h o g a n h j t t a a
q t u x r p a l r e v r
s e s k y s c r a p e r
w n e s t b k c i e h a
a t z y c a s t l e u c
m v a p a r t m e n t k
d n u e f t o i r e a s

hut	nest	hive	tent
cave	tepee	house	shack
hogan	castle	apartment	trailer
skyscraper			barracks

Fix the Leak

Directions: Help the plumber find the sink. Then, color the picture.

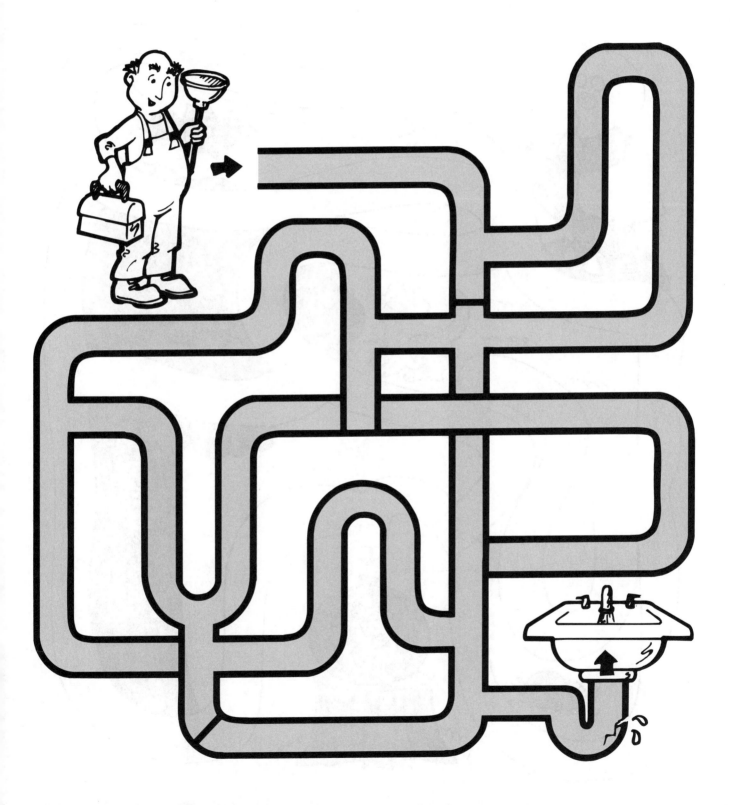

Find the Jack-o'-Lantern

Directions: Help the child get to the jack-o'-lantern.

Cinderella

Directions: Connect the dots from **28** to **92**. Then, color to finish the picture.

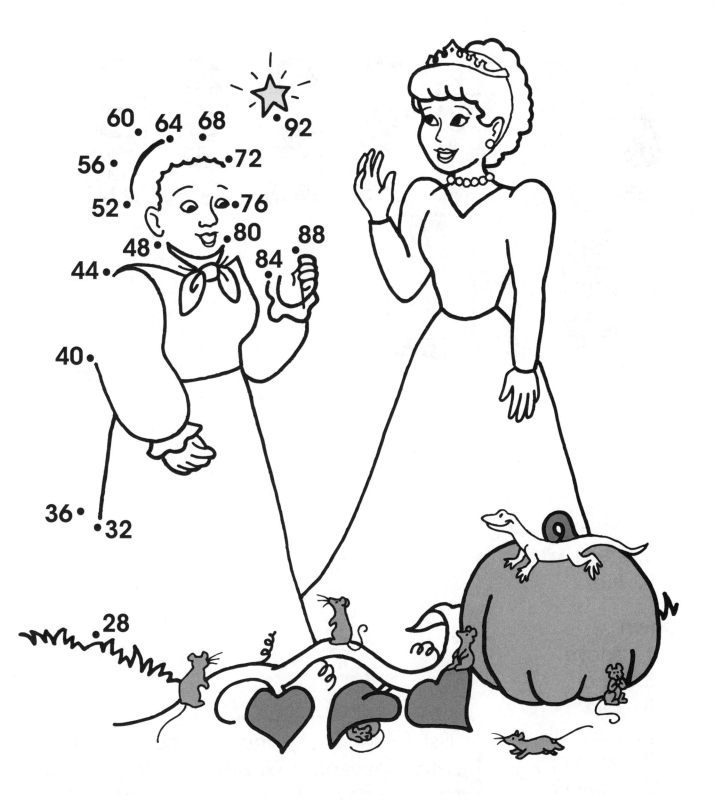

Places, Everyone!

Directions: Use the Word Box and the pictures below to help you fill in the puzzle.

Across
- **2.** frog
- **4.** flower
- **6.** tree
- **9.** sun

Down
- **1.** snake
- **3.** bear
- **5.** rain
- **6.** bird
- **7.** squirrel
- **8.** butterfly

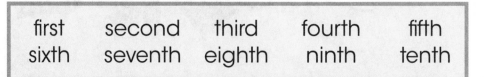

first	second	third	fourth	fifth
sixth	seventh	eighth	ninth	tenth

A Busy Farmer

Directions: Help the farmer find the apples. Then, color the picture.

Boats

Directions: Find and circle the words in the puzzle.

f	a	d	s	t	a	r	b	o	a	r	d	
c	n	b	o	o	m	g	z	k	r	b	s	
o	c	a	l	w	h	e	e	l	u	f	a	
m	h	r	n	t	l	x	m	y	d	k	i	
p	o	g	t	g	c	e	a	j	d	q	l	
a	r	e	u	n	a	b	s	t	e	r	n	
s	h	i	p	p	o	r	t	h	r	i	p	
s	p	o	g	k	b	g	l	t	u	g	r	

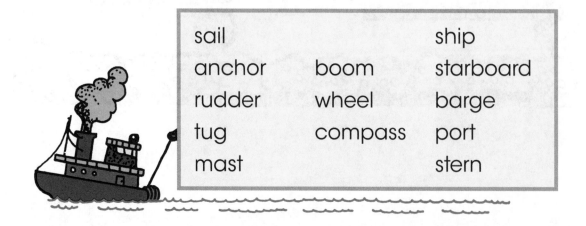

sail		ship
anchor	boom	starboard
rudder	wheel	barge
tug	compass	port
mast		stern

Lynn the Luna Moth

Directions: Connect the dots from **0** to **190**. Then, color to finish the picture.

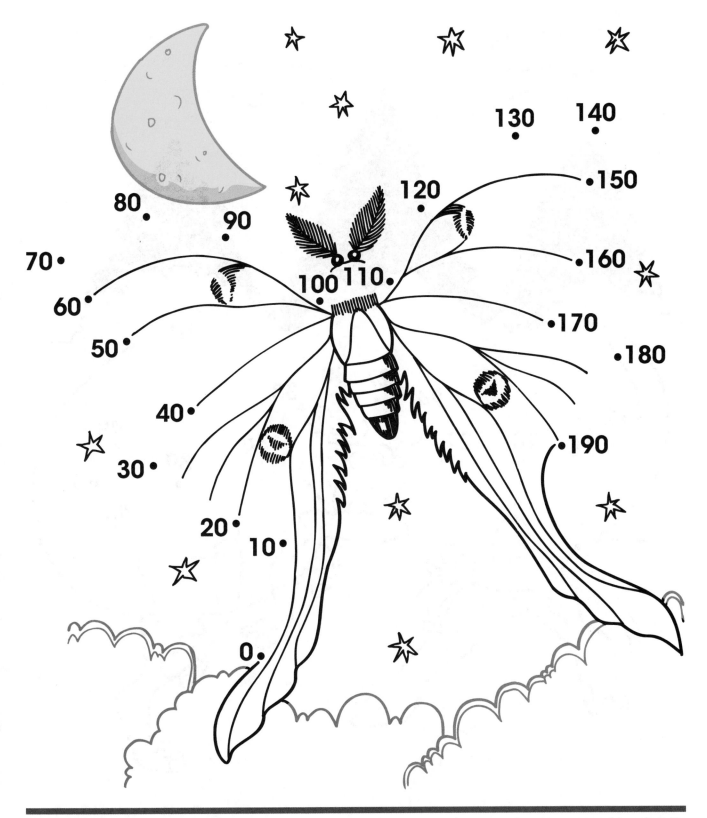

Back in Time

Directions: Connect the dots from **12** to **51**. Then, color to finish the picture.

Ride It

Directions: Color the spaces with things you can ride in or on.

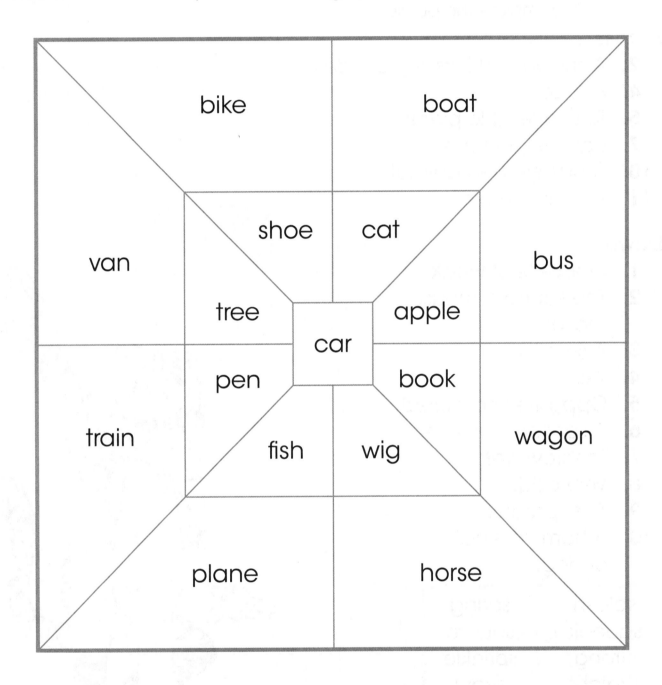

bike

boat

shoe

cat

van

bus

tree

apple

car

pen

book

train

wagon

fish

wig

plane

horse

Stretch!

Directions: Read the clues and use the words in the Word Box to complete the puzzle.

Across

2. A shape that has equal sides.
4. A road.
5. To scatter little pieces.
7. Lightweight rope.
10. A bushy-tailed animal.
11. A stalk of grain.

Down

1. Opposite of **weak**.
2. The sound a mouse makes.
3. A small river.
4. Yell.
5. Opposite of **crooked**.
6. A season of the year.
7. To throw water.
8. Very odd.
9. To separate.
10. A homeless cat or dog.

splash	spring
squeak	square
strong	sprinkle
straight	straw
split	string
scream	squirrel
strange	stream
street	stray

Ages 7+

Happy Birthday

Directions: Help the candles find the cake. Then, color the picture.

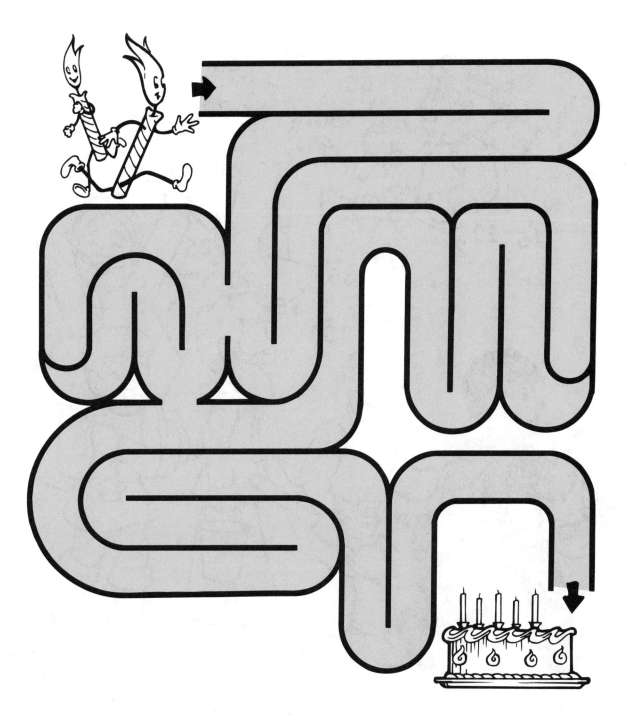

The Seven Dwarfs

Directions: Connect the dots from **15** to **100**. Then, color to finish the picture.

Machines

Directions: Find and circle the words in the puzzle.

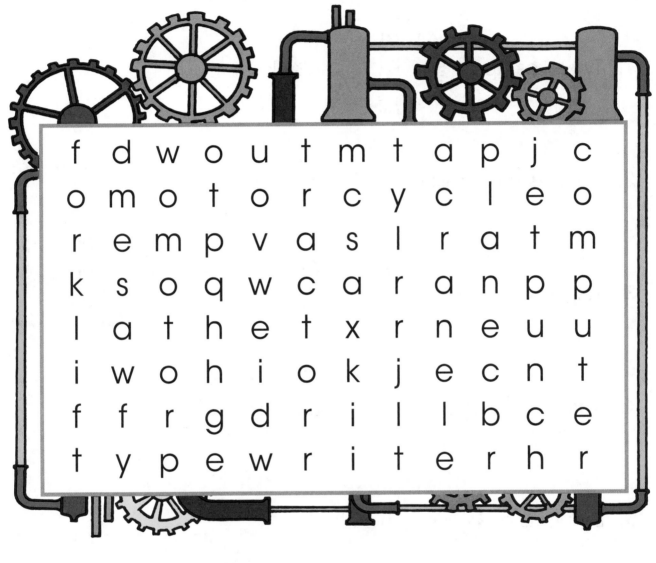

```
f d w o u t m t a p j c
o m o t o r c y c l e o
r e m p v a s l r a t m
k s o q w c a r a n p p
l a t h e t x r n e u u
i w o h i o k j e c n t
f f r g d r i l l b c e
t y p e w r i t e r h r
```

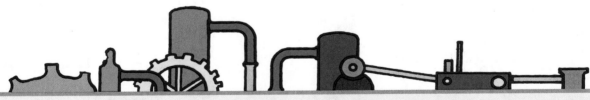

car	drill	crane	tractor	computer
plane	typewriter	saw	motor	punch
motorcycle	jet	lathe	forklift	

Check the Time

Directions: Read about Ty's day. Then, write the times in the puzzle.

1. Ty wakes up at  o'clock.

2. He eats breakfast at  o'clock.

3. Ty goes to school at  o'clock.

5:00
6:00
3:00
8:00
7:00

4. Karate class is at  o'clock.

5. Dinner is at  o'clock.

1.		:	
2.		:	
3.		:	
4.		:	
5.		:	

In the Community

Directions: Read each story. Then, circle the best title.

1. Sara and Jenny put on their old clothes. They painted the fence. They swept the walkway. They worked hard.

Helping Out　　　　**Time to Play**

2. The families took their old things to the park. They had a big sale. They gave the money to the Children's Center.

Family Fun　　　　**A Big Sale**

3. Happy Town had a big fair. There were games and rides for the kids. Everyone had a good time!

Fun at the Fair　　　　**Time to Vote**

4. Hill Town wanted its own community center. The people raised money. When they had enough, they built the center.

Our Community Center　　　　**The Big Fire**

A Treasure Chest

Directions: Help the octopus open the treasure chest.

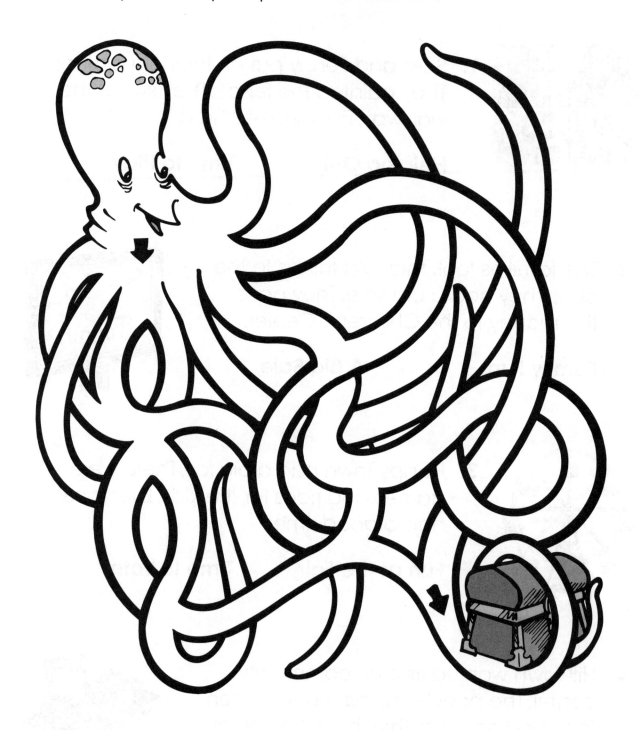

Lost Collar

Directions: Help the puppy find its collar.

Sara the Swallowtail Butterfly

Directions: Connect the dots from **0** to **85**. Then, color to finish the picture.

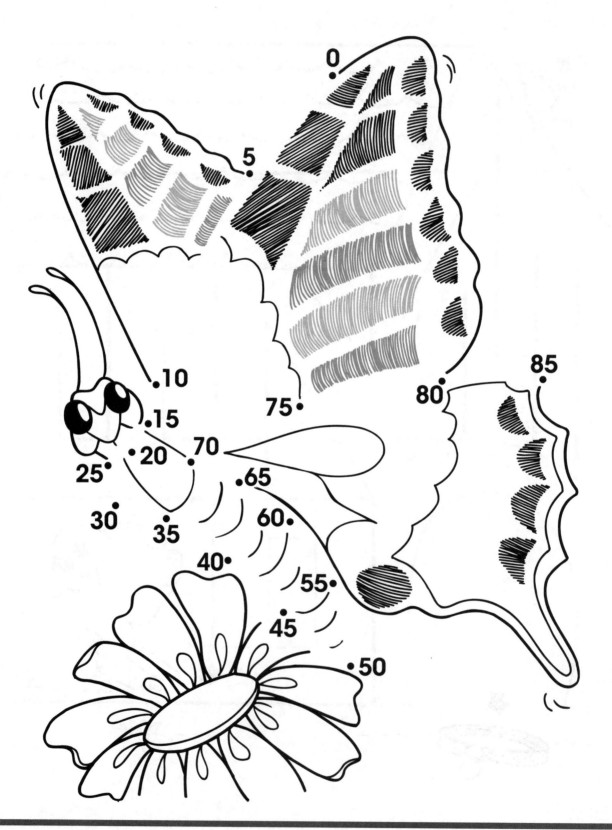

Fill It Up!

Directions: Color the pictures to show **full** and **half-full**.

This cup is **full** of water.

This cup is **half-full** of water.

This pint is **full** of chocolate milk.

This pint is **half-full** of chocolate milk.

This quart is **full** of lemonade.

This quart is **half-full** of lemonade.

This gallon is **full** of orange juice.

This gallon is **half-full** of orange juice.

Which of these drinks would you like to have?

_____

Mary the Millipede

Directions: Connect the dots from **0** to **40**. Then, color to finish the picture.

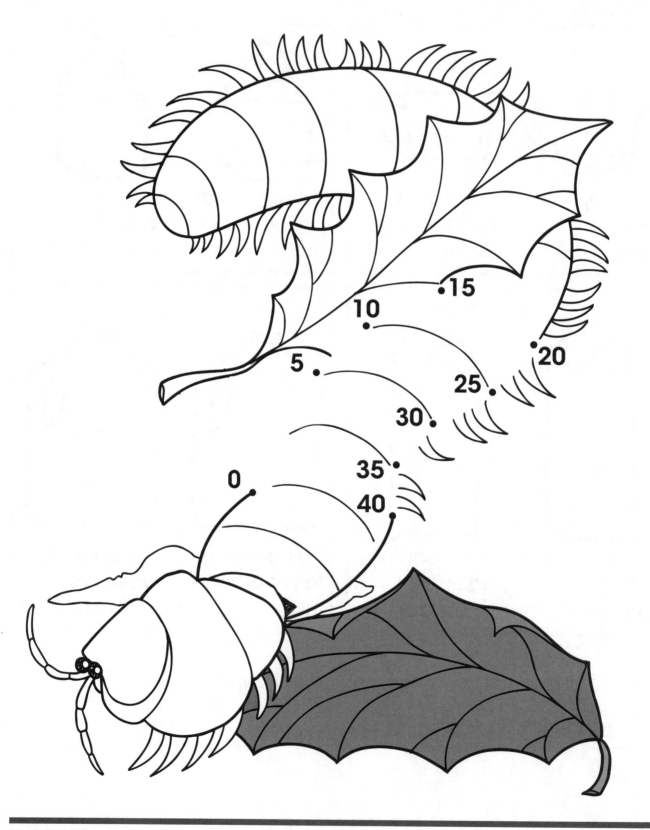

Mystery Picture

Directions: Read each sentence and cross out the picture. What picture is left?

1. It is not Earth.

2. It is not an astronaut.

3. It is not a shuttle.

4. It is not a helmet.

5. It is not a satellite.

6. It is not a rover.

7. It is not the moon.

The mystery picture is a _____ .

The Frog Prince

Directions: Connect the dots from **4** to **28**. Then, color to finish the picture.

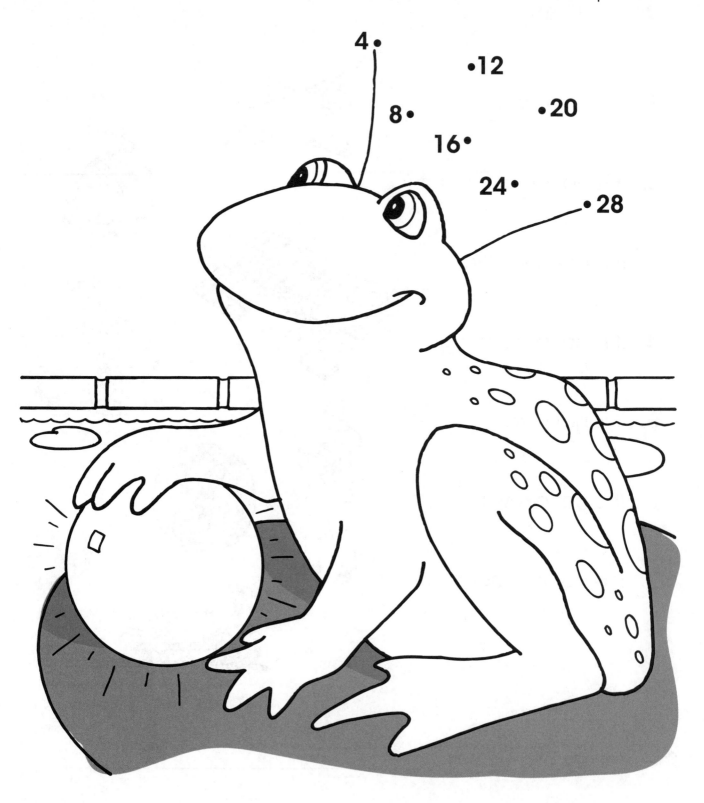

A Gingerbread House

Directions: Connect the dots from **0** to **30**. Then, color to finish the picture.

Irene the Io Moth

Directions: Connect the dots from **25** to **100**. Then, color to finish the picture.

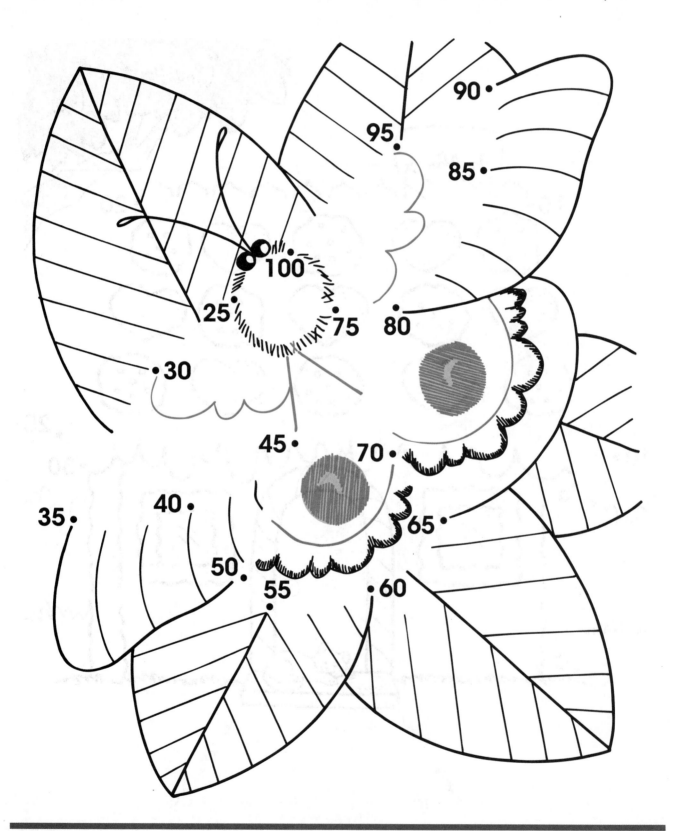

Alison Alligator

Directions: Connect the dots from **1** to **40**. Then, color to finish the picture.

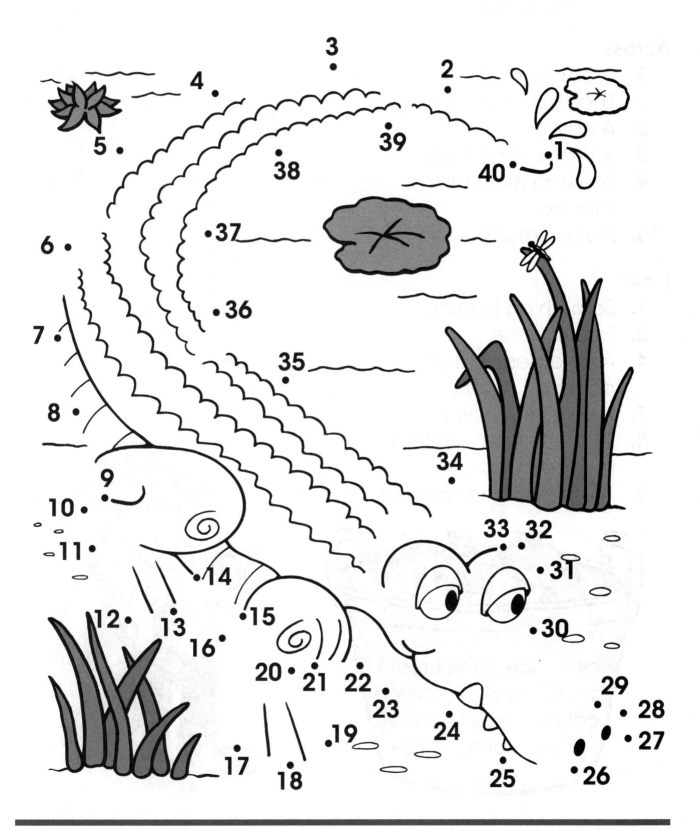

Cool Cider

Directions: Read the clues and use the words in the Word Box to complete the puzzle.

Across

3. A baby's bed.
5. The cost of something.
6. A castle.
8. A yellow vegetable.
9. You can mold things with this.
10. A very small house.

Down

1. Something to drink.
2. Frozen water.
4. A cold dessert that comes in a cone.
7. A very large town.
8. A desert animal with a humped back.
9. A line that goes around.

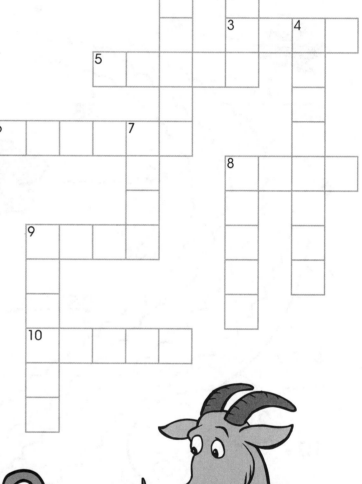

city   ice   ice cream
corn   circle   palace
cabin   clay   camel
price   crib   juice

Oscar the Owlet Moth

Directions: Connect the dots from **0** to **90**. Then, color to finish the picture.

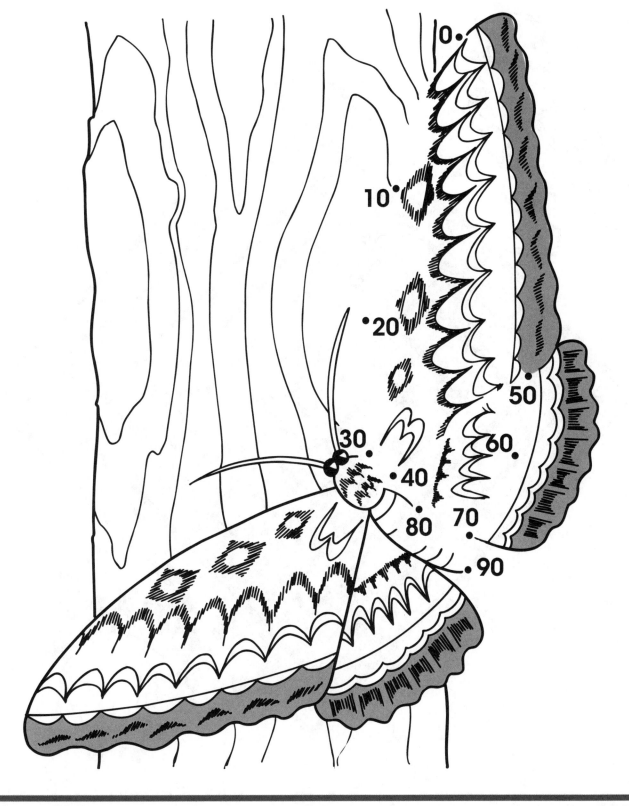

Where's the Turkey?

Directions: Help the Pilgrim boy find the turkey. Then, color the picture.

Water Sports

Directions: Find and circle the words in the puzzle.

```
r o p e s d p a d d l e
w e p u p k s q t x s c
e r o w e t s u i t k i
i f l o a t m a s k i o
g f o l r p v l j n i q
h d i v i n g u w i n m
t h o x y g e n n f g g
s w i m m i n g b e z a
```

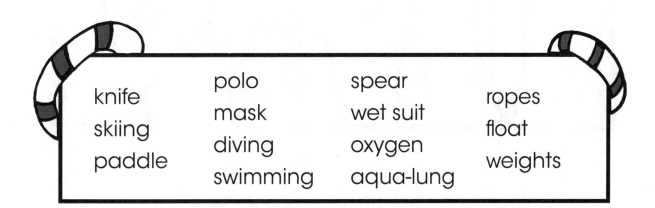

knife
skiing
paddle

polo
mask
diving
swimming

spear
wet suit
oxygen
aqua-lung

ropes
float
weights

Find the Worm

Directions: Help the bird reach the worm.

Rapunzel

Directions: Connect the dots from **5** to **70**. Then, color to finish the picture.

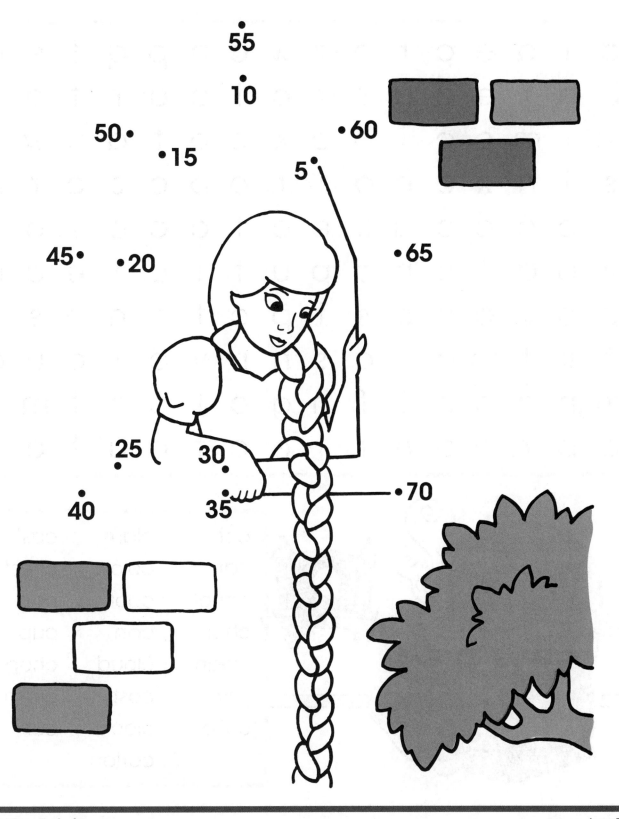

Careful!

Directions: Find and circle the words in the puzzle.

```
d i o e c r b z w c n p q t e a
b h j e c a r r o t c o r f g i
m r m c c l o c k c o f d u w j
s i n x c h a i r o b c s c r h
a c c c c a k e c t c c o l o r
v o a l c h o p u t i c l e a n
p o s a c o s t p o t c h e s t
t k t m c r a s h n y c l o u d
m n b c o t f h g o t c a t m s
c b r c a n j i e c t c u t o e
```

cot	clam	cast
cat	color	chest
carrot	cook	cob
chair	can	cup
clean	cloud	chop
city	cost	crash
cake	clock	cut
	cotton	

Find the Mystery Number

Directions: Color the spaces with words that name shapes or colors **red**. Color the spaces with words that name numbers **purple**.

nine	circle	one	rectangle	fifteen
seven	red	nineteen	blue	eleven
two	octagon	twenty	hexagon	eighteen
eight	green	star	yellow	heart
one	thirteen	twelve	rhombus	ten
three	six	seventeen	brown	five
thirteen	fourteen	four	square	sixteen

The mystery number is _____.

A Happy Hummingbird

Directions: Help the hummingbird get to the flowers. Then, color the picture.

The Beast

Directions: Connect the dots from **8** to **52**. Then, color to finish the picture.

28
24
32
20
8
12
16
36
40
48
44
52

A Perky Penguin

Directions: Help the mother penguin find the baby penguin.

Patterns

Directions: Color the spaces with short vowel words **green**. Color the spaces with long vowel words yellow.

tree / black	hand	wig	cake / fox
time / green	rain / ant	egg / ice	gate / mule
sock / name	gum	mop	bat / boat

The Wild West

Directions: Color the spaces with long vowel words **brown**. Color the spaces with short vowel words **blue**.

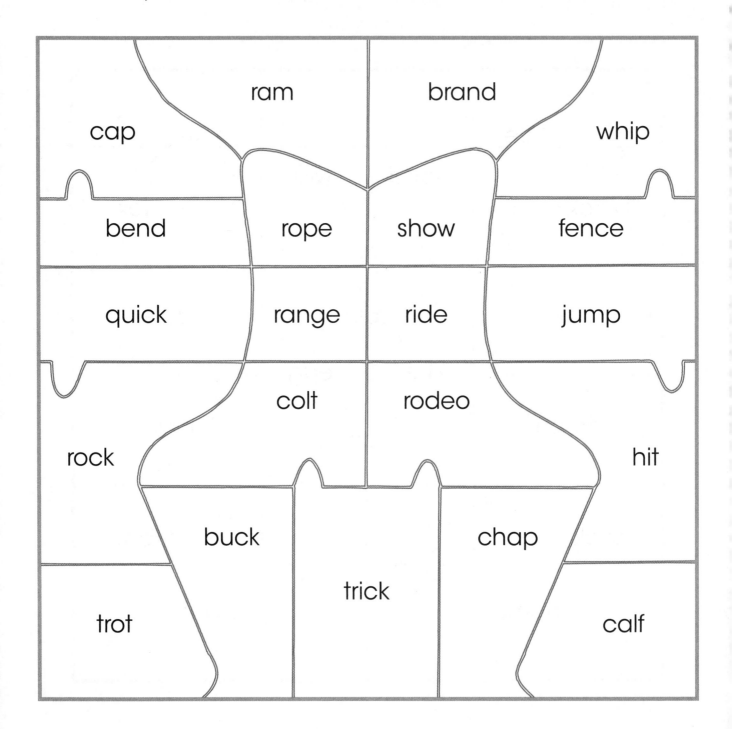

ram

brand

cap

whip

bend

rope

show

fence

quick

range

ride

jump

colt

rodeo

rock

hit

buck

chap

trick

trot

calf

What did you color? _____

Compound Fun

Directions: Match each word in the Word Box with a word in the puzzle to make a new word.

cake	shine	knob	room
port	shore	ball	fish

1. | s | e | a | | | | |

2. | a | i | r | | | |

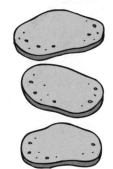

3. | p | a | n | | | | |

4. | s | u | n | | | | |

5. | d | o | o | r | | | |

6. | b | a | t | h | | | |

7. | f | o | o | t | | | |

8. | g | o | l | d | | |

Where's the Glove?

Directions: Help the players find the baseball glove.

Goldilocks

Directions: Connect the dots from **36** to **80**. Then, color to finish the picture.

40

44

48

36 80

76

56 52

72

60

68 64

Rocks and Minerals

Directions: Find and circle the words in the puzzle.

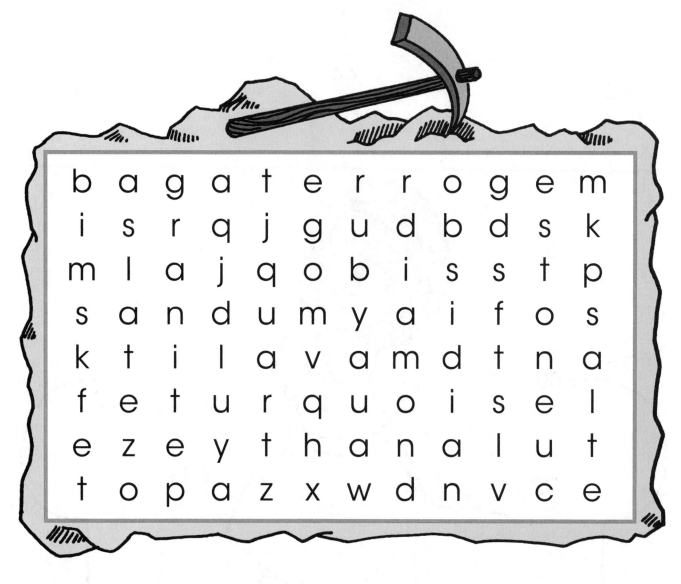

```
b a g a t e r r o g e m
i s r q j g u d b d s k
m l a j q o b i s s t p
s a n d u m y a i f o s
k t i l a v a m d t n a
f e t u r q u o i s e l
e z e y t h a n a l u t
t o p a z x w d n v c e
```

slate
agate
salt
granite
obsidian

gem
lava
sand
stone

ruby
topaz
quartz
diamond
turquoise

Hansel and Gretel

Directions: Connect the dots from **4** to **32**. Then, color to finish the picture.

Ages 7+

Shining Bright

Directions: To find the mystery letter, color the spaces with the following letters **red**.

Q F V P G O M N U S

Q	G	M	N
S	A	J	W
U	F	P	H
O	L	T	Z
V	Y	R	B

Circle the mystery letter.   E   F   P

Birds

Directions: Find and circle the words in the puzzle.

```
c h i c k a d e e a c h g
i j k d a e a g l e s d o
o n b l u w s w a n p f o
d w c m x c u t b i a e s
e f l g y v k p a r r o t
h p e n g u i n s r r j r
w o o d p e c k e r o k i
z f l a m i n g o l w n c
b l u e b i r d q m p o h
```

chickadee	parrot	eagle
sparrow	owl	flamingo
bluebird	duck	ostrich
woodpecker	penguin	swan

Geography

Directions: Find and circle the words in the puzzle.

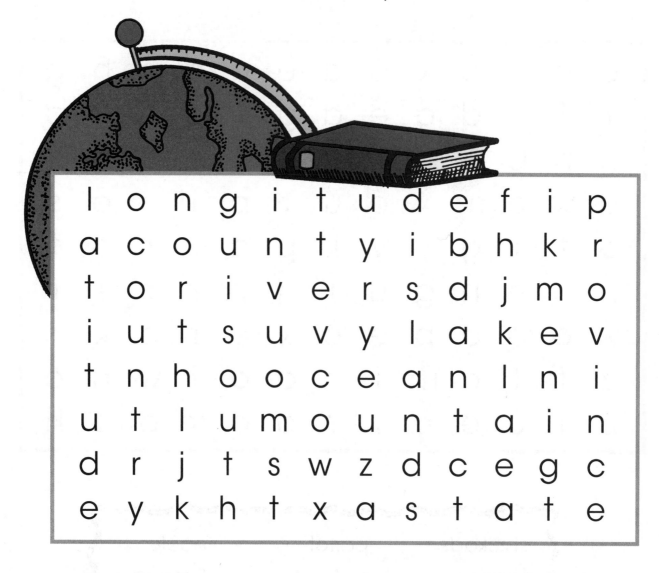

```
l o n g i t u d e f i p
a c o u n t y i b h k r
t o r i v e r s d j m o
i u t s u v y l a k e v
t n h o o c e a n l n i
u t l u m o u n t a i n
d r j t s w z d c e g c
e y k h t x a s t a t e
```

state
latitude
country
longitude

lake
river
north
ocean
mountain

south
island
county
province

A Prince and a Princess

Directions: Help the prince get to the princess. Then, color the picture.

Mammals

Directions: Find and circle the words in the puzzle.

```
a c h i m p a n z e e c a
d b e l g j n g i d b r z
o w d f i k t h f e c a t
l c h h w s e a l d y c v
p u z a y x a j k o x c w
h t v a l n t i a g f o t
i s p r o e e m p p u o s
n b a t j n r o e q r n x
l h m i k p o r p o i s e
```

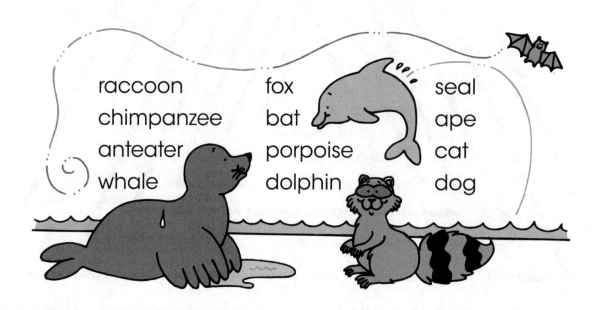

raccoon   fox   seal

chimpanzee   bat   ape

anteater   porpoise cat

whale   dolphin dog

Ride the Wave

Directions: Help the surfer reach the boy on the beach.

Going Places

Directions: Read the clues and use the words in the Word Box to complete the puzzle.

Word Box:
airplane
train
bike
bus
car
truck
boat
horse
balloon

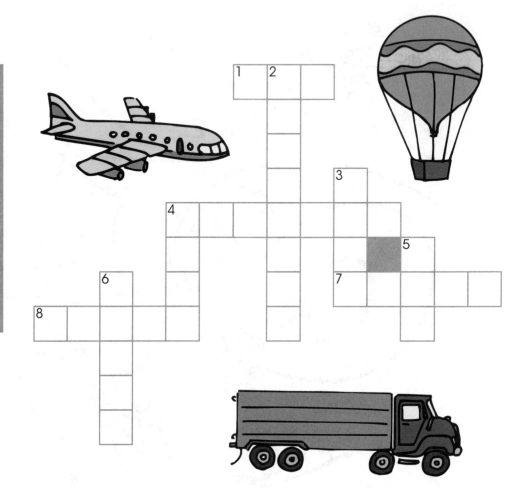

Across

1. It is an automobile.
4. Hot air makes it rise into the sky.
7. This can carry heavy loads on the road.
8. It has a saddle.

Down

2. This flies people from city to city.
3. This carries people and big loads on water.
4. It has two wheels and pedals.
5. This takes many people around the city.
6. It runs on tracks.

Gina the Goliath Beetle

Directions: Connect the dots from **5** to **50**. Then, color to finish the picture.

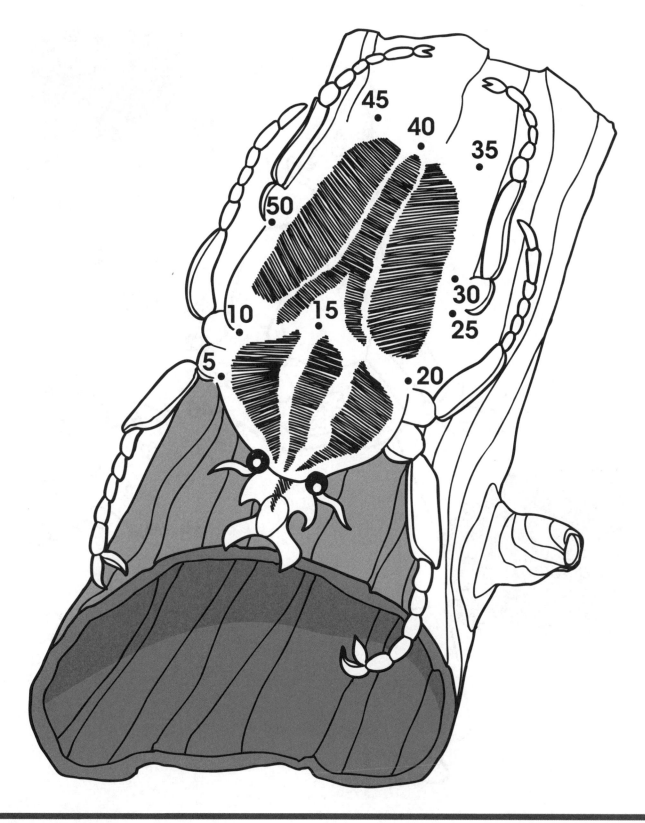

Beauty

Directions: Connect the dots from **4** to **48**. Then, color to finish the picture.

Walter the Water Bug

Directions: Connect the dots from **0** to **70**. Then, color to finish the picture.

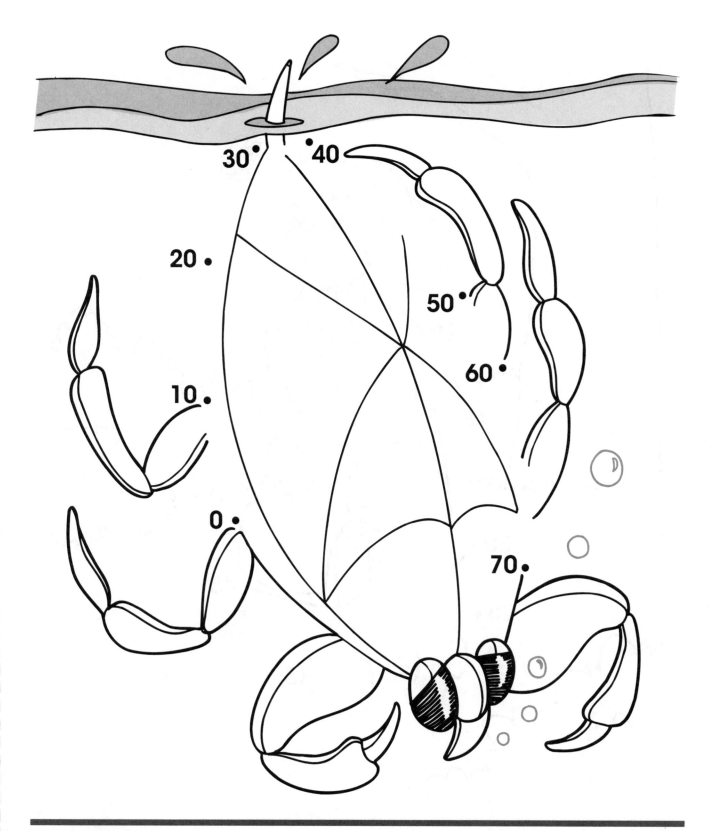

Red Riding Hood

Directions: Connect the dots from **10** to **45**. Then, color to finish the picture.

10 •
15 •
20 •
25 •
30
35
40
45

Clean-up Time

Directions: Help the boy get to the shopping cart. Then, color the picture.

Candy Store Patterns

Directions: Look at the patterns. Draw in each missing piece of candy.

1.

2.

3.

4.

5.

6.

7.

8.

Kaori Kangaroo

Directions: Connect the dots from **1** to **50**. Then, color to finish the picture.

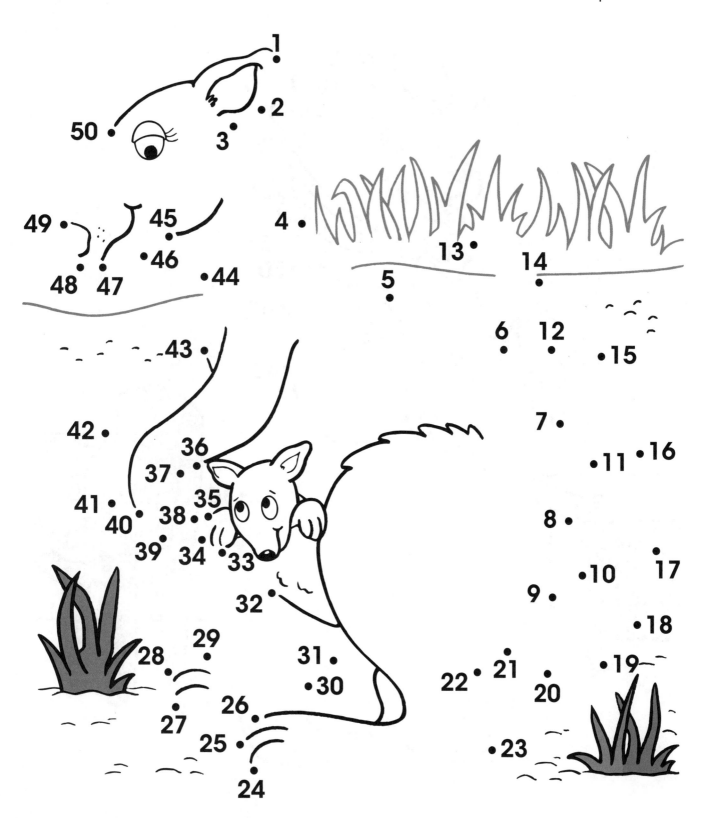

Big Bad Wolf

Directions: Connect the dots from **10** to **55**. Then, color to finish the picture.

Reptiles

Directions: Find and circle the words in the puzzle.

```
a r a t t l e s n a k e c
l c r o c o d i l e z a h
l t o r t o i s e l i n a
i d u w x a k j g i g a m
g e y r v o l n e z u c e
a t s u t p m g c a a o l
t c b r q l f i k r n n e
o s k i n k e h o d a d o
r s i d e w i n d e r a n
```

turtle   gecko
iguana   skink
crocodile   sidewinder
lizard   chameleon
tortoise   anaconda
alligator   rattlesnake

Hunting for Carrots

Directions: Help the rabbit find the carrots. Then, color the picture.

Answer Key

5

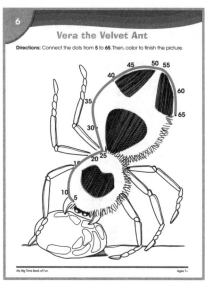

6

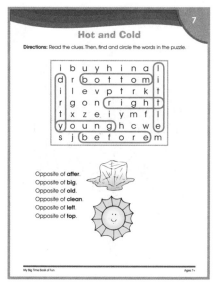

7

8

9

10

Answer Key

11

12

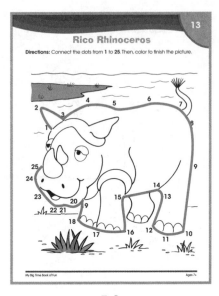

13

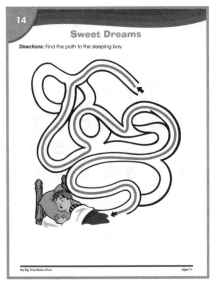

14

15

Mail Call

Directions: Unscramble the words that have to do with mail. Use the words in the Word Box to help you.

1. rettles l e t t e r s
2. cpageksa p a c k a g e s
3. tpamss s t a m p s
4. ilam rrcaire m a i l   c a r r i e r
5. tsop oceiff p o s t   o f f i c e
6. axombli m a i l b o x
7. leeydivr d e l i v e r y
8. dracs c a r d s

delivery	mail carrier	
letters	stamps	packages
mailbox	cards	post office

16

Answer Key

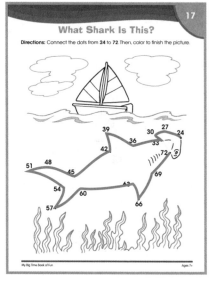

17

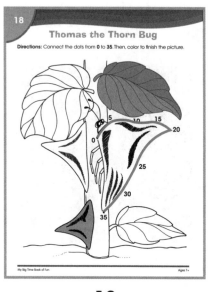

18

19

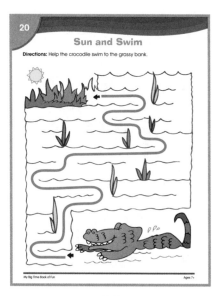

20

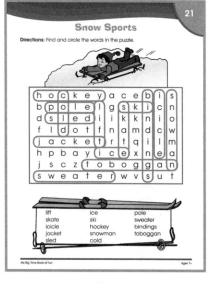

21

22

Answer Key

23

24

25

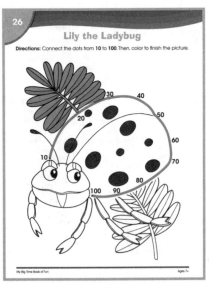

26

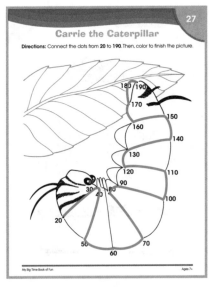

27

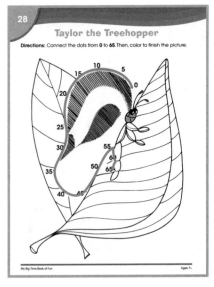

28

Answer Key

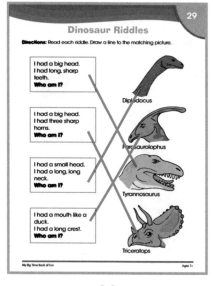

29

30

31

32

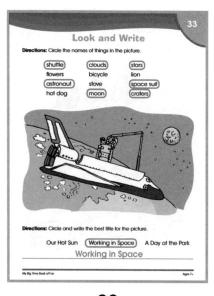

33

34

Answer Key

35

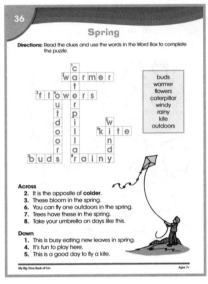

36

37

38

39

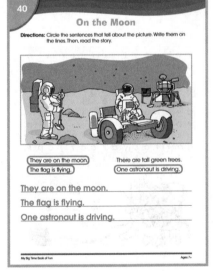

40

Answer Key

41

42

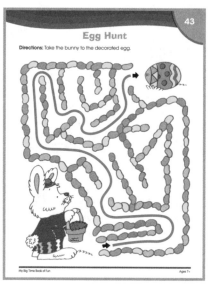

43

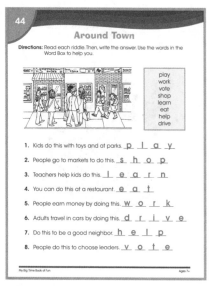

44

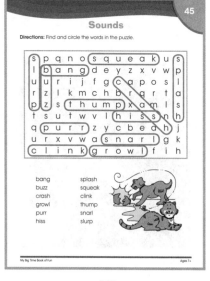

45

46

Answer Key

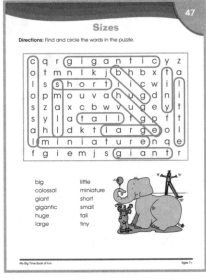

47

Sizes

Directions: Find and circle the words in the puzzle.

c	q	r	g	i	g	a	n	t	i	c	y	z
o	t	m	n	l	k	j	b	h	b	x	t	a
l	s	s	h	o	r	t	l	i	c	w	i	l
o	p	m	o	u	v	a	h	u	g	d	n	l
s	z	a	x	c	b	w	v	u	g	e	y	l
s	y	l	a	t	a	l	l	f	g	p	f	l
a	h	l	d	k	t	l	a	r	g	e	o	l
l	m	i	n	i	a	t	u	r	e	n	q	e
f	g	i	e	m	j	s	g	i	a	n	t	r

big	little
colossal	miniature
giant	short
gigantic	small
huge	tall
large	tiny

47

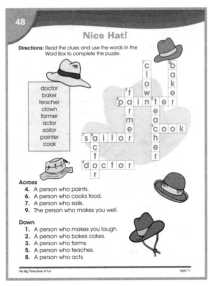

48

Nice Hat!

Directions: Read the clues and use the words in the Word Box to complete the puzzle.

Word Box:
doctor
baker
teacher
clown
farmer
actor
sailor
painter
cook

Across
4. A person who paints.
6. A person who cooks food.
7. A person who sails.
9. The person who makes you well.

Down
1. A person who makes you laugh.
2. A person who bakes cakes.
3. A person who farms.
5. A person who teaches.
8. A person who acts.

48

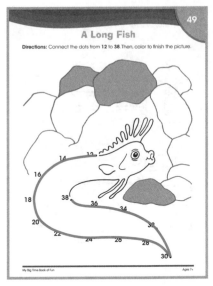

49

A Long Fish

Directions: Connect the dots from **12** to **38**. Then, color to finish the picture.

49

50

Who Is Bigger?

Directions: Help the bear get home. Color numbers greater than **10**.

50

51

What Is It?

Directions: Color the spaces with words that name vehicles yellow. Color the other spaces blue.

51

52

A Cold Place

Directions: Help the polar bear find the North Pole.

52

Answer Key

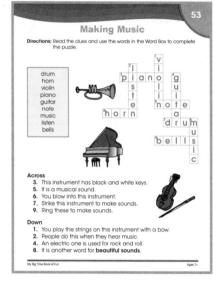

53

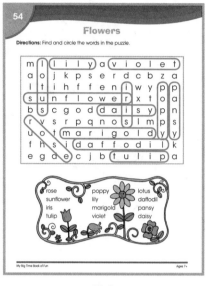

54

55

56

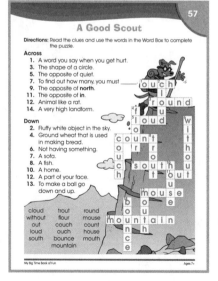

57

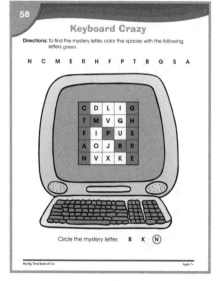

58

Answer Key

59 — Camping Time

Directions: Help the Boy Scout find the tent. Then, color the picture.

59

60 — The Gingerbread Man

Directions: Connect the dots from **0** to **24**. Then, color to finish the picture.

60

61 — Moving to Music

Directions: Read the clues and use the words in the Word Box to complete the puzzle.

Word Box: stretch, move, dance, leap, glide, step, skip, whirl, pose

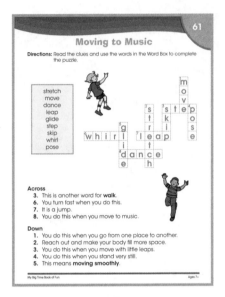

Across
3. This is another word for **walk**.
6. You turn fast when you do this.
7. It is a jump.
8. You do this when you move to music.

Down
1. You do this when you go from one place to another.
2. Reach out and make your body fill more space.
3. You do this when you move with little leaps.
4. You do this when you stand very still.
5. This means **moving smoothly**.

61

62 — A Smart Coral

Directions: Connect the dots from **9** to **54**. Then, color to finish the picture.

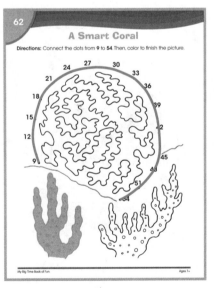

62

63 — Read All About It

Directions: Read the clues and use the words in the Word Box to complete the puzzle.

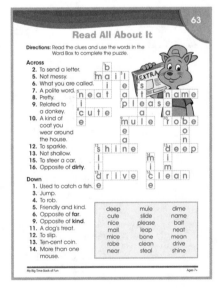

Across
2. To send a letter.
5. Not messy.
6. What you are called.
7. A polite word.
8. Pretty.
9. Related to a donkey.
10. A kind of coat you wear around the house.
12. To sparkle.
13. Not shallow.
15. To steer a car.
16. Opposite of **dirty**.

Down
1. Used to catch a fish.
3. Jump.
4. To rob.
5. Friendly and kind.
6. Opposite of **far**.
9. Opposite of **kind**.
11. A dog's treat.
12. To slip.
13. Ten-cent coin.
14. More than one mouse.

Word Box: deep, cute, nice, mail, mice, robe, near, mule, slide, please, leap, bone, clean, steal, dime, name, bait, neat, mean, drive, shine

63

64 — An Unsafe Ride

Directions: Help the girl find the helmet.

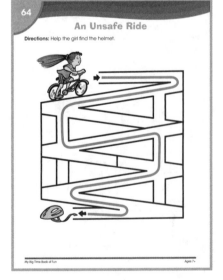

64

Answer Key

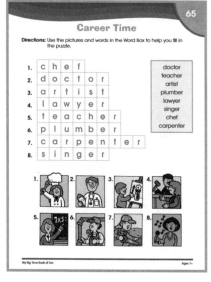

Career Time (65)

Directions: Use the pictures and words in the Word Box to help you fill in the puzzle.

1. chef
2. doctor
3. artist
4. lawyer
5. teacher
6. plumber
7. carpenter
8. singer

Word Box: doctor, teacher, artist, plumber, lawyer, singer, chef, carpenter

65

Unscramble Time (66)

Directions: Unscramble each word. Be sure it goes with the meaning.

1. One who plays is called a lapeyr **player**.
2. A round thing you can kick is a lalb **ball**.
3. A sweet treat to eat is danyc **candy**.
4. Something you can win is a pzire **prize**.
5. A person who wins is the rnnewi **winner**.
6. One who sails a boat is a ailsor **sailor**.

Word Box: prize, winner, player, ball, sailor, candy

66

Laughable Fellow (67)

Directions: Read the clues and use the words in the Word Box to complete the puzzle.

Word Box: breakable, widen, readable, sinkable, harden, lighten, soften, washable, darken, enjoyable, written, straighten

Across
2. Opposite of darken.
4. To make wider.
5. Can be sunk.
7. To make hard.
8. Can be read.
11. Can be broken.

Down
1. Put in writing.
3. To make something not crooked.
4. Can be washed.
6. A lot of fun.
9. To make darker.
10. Opposite of harden.

67

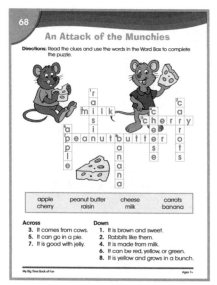

An Attack of the Munchies (68)

Directions: Read the clues and use the words in the Word Box to complete the puzzle.

Word Box: apple, cherry, peanut butter, raisin, cheese, milk, carrots, banana

Across
3. It comes from cows.
5. It can go in a pie.
7. It is good with jelly.

Down
1. It is brown and sweet.
2. Rabbits like them.
4. It is made from milk.
6. It can be red, yellow, or green.
8. It is yellow and grows in a bunch.

68

Snow White (69)

Directions: Connect the dots from 25 to 100. Then, color to finish the picture.

69

Ticket, Please! (70)

Directions: Find and circle the words in the puzzle.

zero, one, two, three, four, five, six, seven, eight, nine, ten, eleven

70

Answer Key

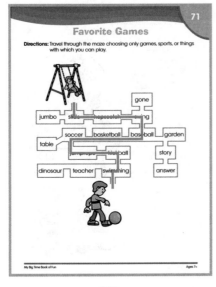

71

72

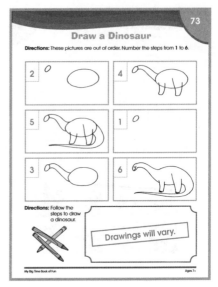

73

74

75

76

Answer Key

77

Nuts, Seeds, and Beans

Directions: Find and circle the words in the puzzle.

peanut   pea   pistachio
almond   pecan   coconut
soybean   pod   chestnut
lima   walnut   cashew
macadamia   shell

77

78

Wagon Wheel

Directions: Write the first letter of the words in the puzzle wheel.

78

79

Field Goal

Directions: Kick the football through the goalposts.

79

80

Sharpy Swordfish

Directions: Connect the dots from **3** to **27**. Then, color to finish the picture.

80

81

Feelings

Directions: Find and circle the words in the puzzle.

happy   jealous   angry
sad   loved   hopeful
shy   sorry   surprised
excited   proud   afraid

81

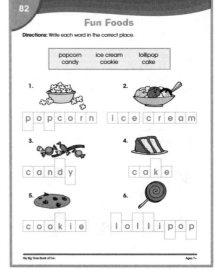

82

Fun Foods

Directions: Write each word in the correct place.

popcorn   ice cream   lollipop
candy   cookie   cake

1. popcorn
2. ice cream
3. candy
4. cake
5. cookie
6. lollipop

82

Answer Key

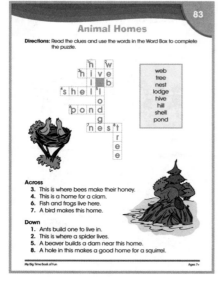

Animal Homes

Directions: Read the clues and use the words in the Word Box to complete the puzzle.

Word Box:
web
tree
nest
lodge
hive
hill
shell
pond

Across
3. This is where bees make their honey.
4. This is a home for a clam.
6. Fish and frogs live here.
7. A bird makes this home.

Down
1. Ants build one to live in.
2. This is where a spider lives.
5. A beaver builds a dam near this home.
8. A hole in this makes a good home for a squirrel.

83

Space Age

Directions: Find and circle the words in the puzzle.

Word list:
radar, star, suit, galaxy, space, air, fuel, clouds, planet, comet, moon, meteor, rocket, television

84

I'm Late

Directions: Help the lady get to the train. Then, color the picture.

85

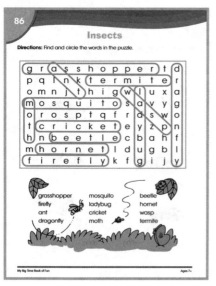

Insects

Directions: Find and circle the words in the puzzle.

Word list:
grasshopper, mosquito, beetle, firefly, ladybug, hornet, ant, cricket, wasp, dragonfly, moth, termite

86

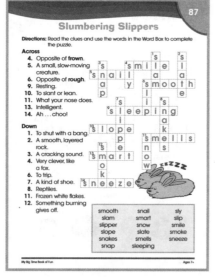

Slumbering Slippers

Directions: Read the clues and use the words in the Word Box to complete the puzzle.

Across
4. Opposite of *frown*.
5. A small, slow-moving creature.
6. Opposite of *rough*.
9. Resting.
10. To slant or lean.
11. What your nose does.
13. Intelligent.
14. Ah . . . choo!

Down
1. To shut with a bang.
2. A smooth, layered rock.
3. A cracking sound.
4. Very clever, like a fox.
6. To trip.
7. A kind of shoe.
8. Reptiles.
11. Frozen white flakes.
12. Something burning gives off.

Word Box:
smooth, snail, sly
slam, smart, slip
slipper, snow, smile
slope, slate, smoke
snakes, smells, sneeze
snap, sleeping

87

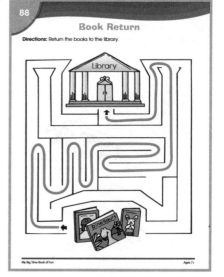

Book Return

Directions: Return the books to the library.

88

Answer Key

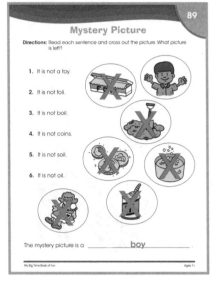

89

90

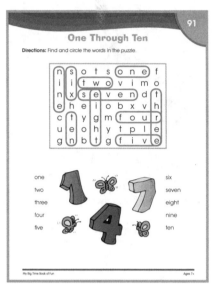

91

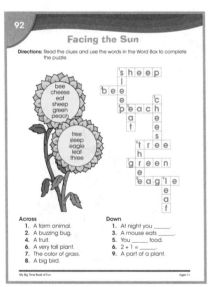

92

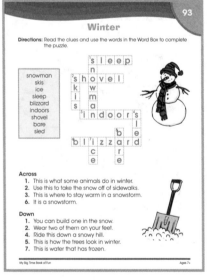

93

94

Answer Key

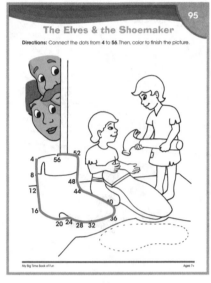

95

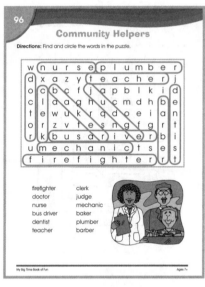

96

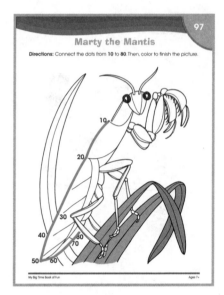

97

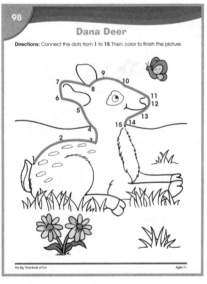

98

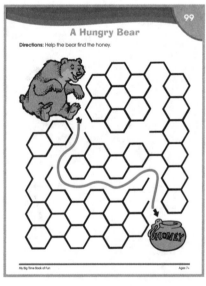

99

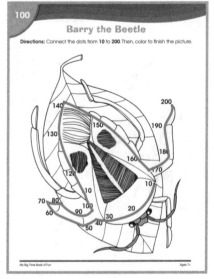

100

Answer Key

101

102

103

104

105

106

Answer Key

107

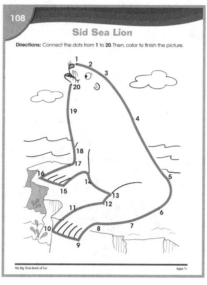

108

109

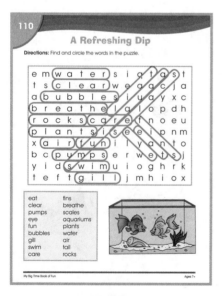

110

111

Holidays

Directions: Write the holidays from the Word Box in the puzzle. Then, find the secret word in the heavy boxes going down.

1. C h r i s t m a s
2. F a t h e r's D a y
3. V a l e n t i n e's D a y
4. I n d e p e n d e n c e D a y
5. A r b o r D a y
6. E a s t e r
7. H a n u k k a h
8. V e t e r a n s D a y
9. M o t h e r's D a y

Mother's Day
Father's Day
Veterans Day
Independence Day
Arbor Day
Christmas
Easter
Valentine's Day
Hanukkah

The secret word is ___Celebrate___

112

Answer Key

113
Free to Be Me!

Directions: Connect the dots from **33** to **90**. Then, color to finish the picture.

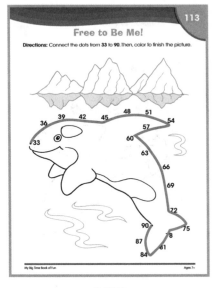

113

114
Let's Share It!

Directions: Color the picture in each row that shows equal parts. Then, write the matching fraction word.

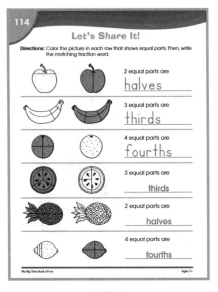

2 equal parts are **halves**

3 equal parts are **thirds**

4 equal parts are **fourths**

3 equal parts are **thirds**

2 equal parts are **halves**

4 equal parts are **fourths**

114

115
Helpful Friends

Directions: Read the clues and use the words in the Word Box to complete the puzzle.

fireman alarm
help careful
accident obey
matches siren
policeman

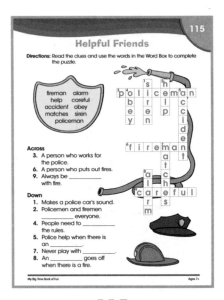

Across
3. A person who works for the police.
6. A person who puts out fires.
9. Always be _____ with fire.

Down
1. Makes a police car's sound.
2. Policemen and firemen _____ everyone.
4. People need to _____ the rules.
5. Police help when there is an _____.
7. Never play with _____.
8. An _____ goes off when there is a fire.

115

116
Plump Pig

Directions: Color each u purple. Then, color the rest of the picture.

116

117
Manny the Mosquito

Directions: Connect the dots from **0** to **110**. Then, color to finish the picture.

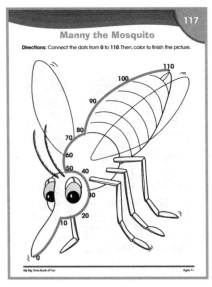

117

118
Around the City

Directions: Read the clues and use the words in the Word Box to complete the puzzle.

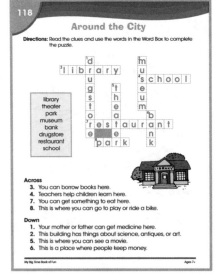

library
theater
park
museum
bank
drugstore
restaurant
school

Across
3. You can borrow books here.
4. Teachers help children learn here.
7. You can get something to eat here.
8. This is where you can go to play or ride a bike.

Down
1. Your mother or father can get medicine here.
2. This building has things about science, antiques, or art.
5. This is where you can see a movie.
6. This is a place where people keep money.

118

Answer Key

119

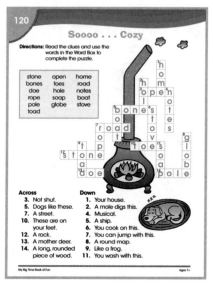

120

121

122

123

124

Answer Key

125

126

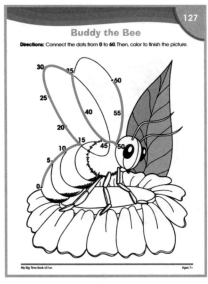

127

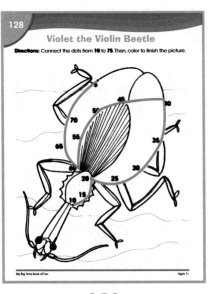

128

129

130

Answer Key

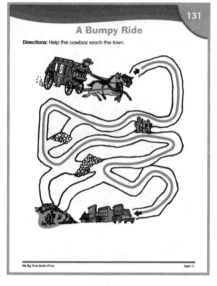

131

132

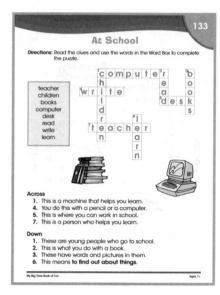

133

134

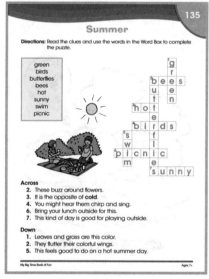

135

136

Answer Key

137

138

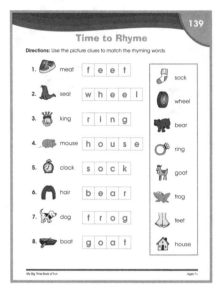

139

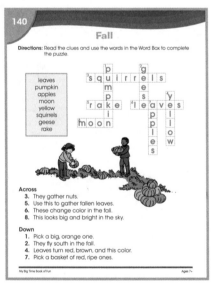

140

141

142

Answer Key

143

144

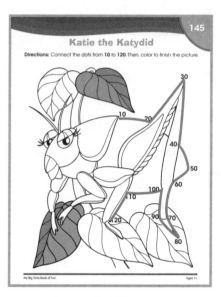

145

146

147

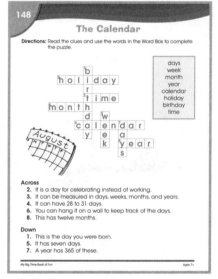

148

Answer Key

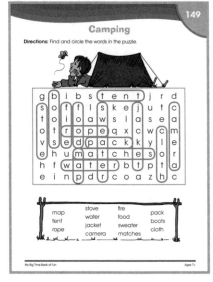

149

150

151

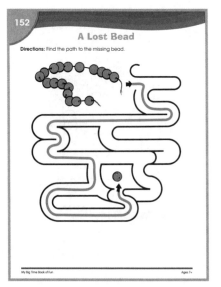

152

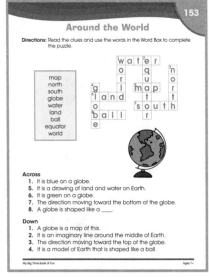

153

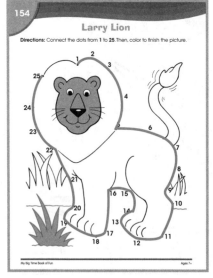

154

Answer Key

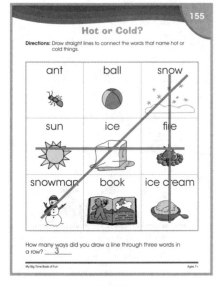

155

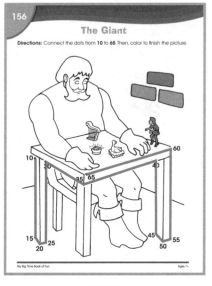

156

157

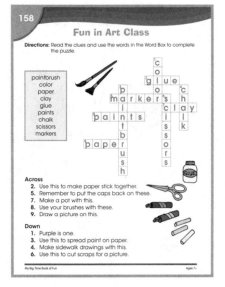

158

159

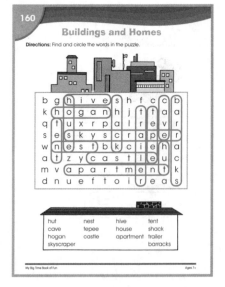

160

Answer Key

161

162

163

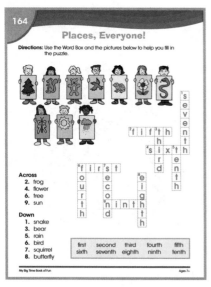

164

165

166

Answer Key

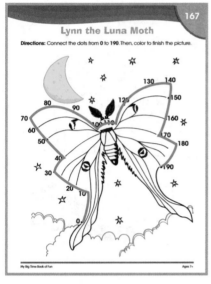

167

168

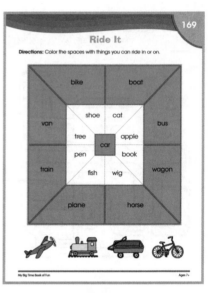

169

170

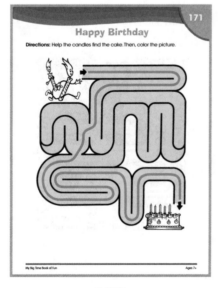

171

172

Answer Key

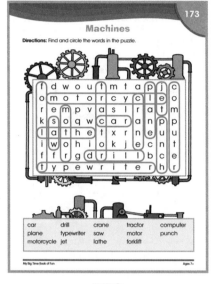

173

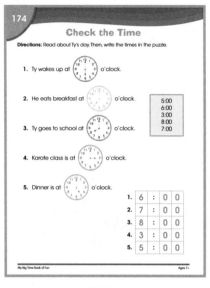

174

175

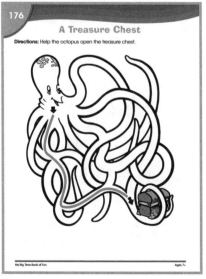

176

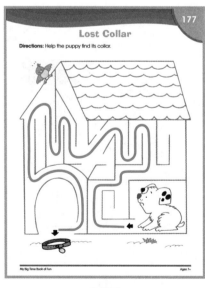

177

178

Answer Key

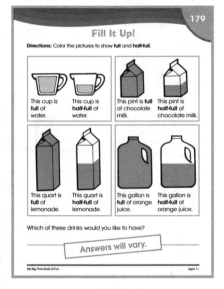

179

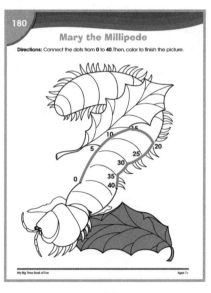

180

181

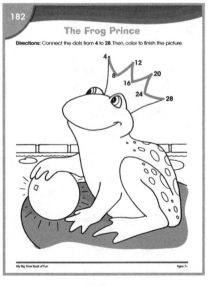

182

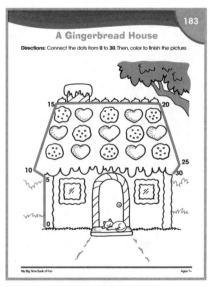

183

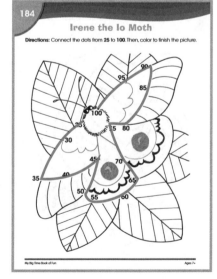

184

Answer Key

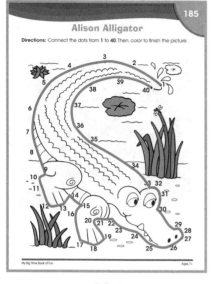

185

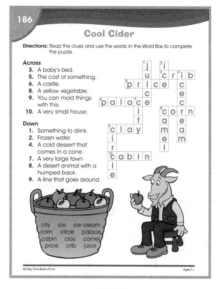

186

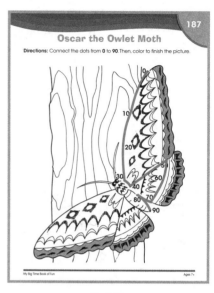

187

188

189

190

Answer Key

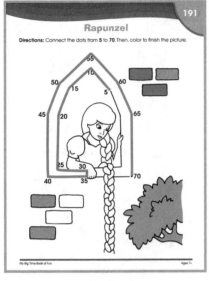

191

192

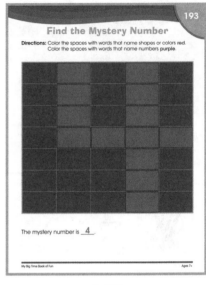

193

194

195

196

Answer Key

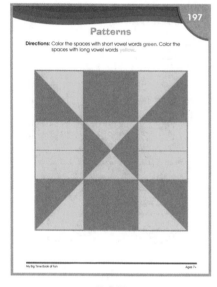

197

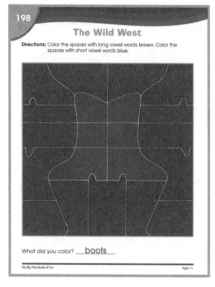

198

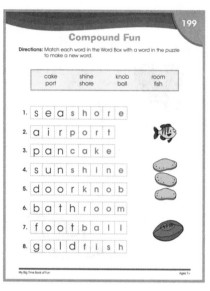

199

200

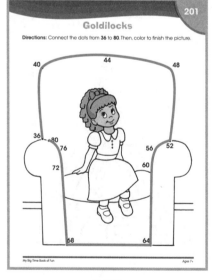

201

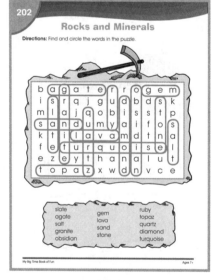

202

Answer Key

203

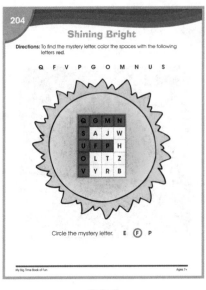

204

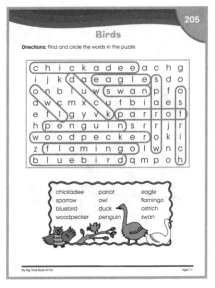

205

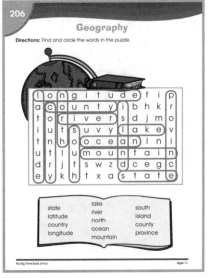

206

207

208

Answer Key

209

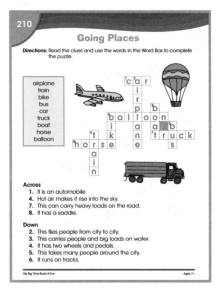

210

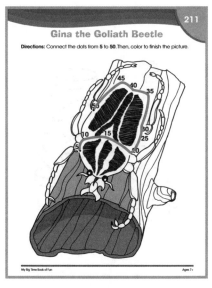

211

212

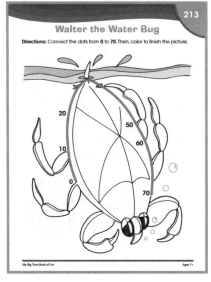

213

214

Answer Key

215

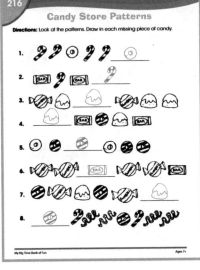

216

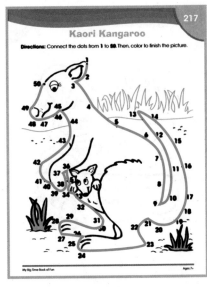

217

218

219

220